Tips for the
LAZY
GARDENER

Linda Tilgner

A Storey Book

Storey Communications, Inc.
Schoolhouse Road
Pownal, Vermont 05261

*The mission of Storey Communications is to serve our customers
by publishing practical information that encourages
personal independence in harmony with the environment.*

Cover design and illustration by Jane Isabella
Text design by Cindy McFarland
Production assistance by Susan Bernier, Eileen Clawson, and
    Erin Lincourt
Illustrations by David Sylvester
Indexed by Susan Olason, Indexes and Knowledge Maps

Printed in the United States by R.R. Donnelley
10 9 8 7 6 5 4 3 2 1

Library of Congress Cataloging-in-Publication Data

Tilgner, Linda, 1937–
    Tips for the lazy gardener / by Linda Tilgner
        p.   cm.
    "A Storey Publishing Book"
    Includes index.
    ISBN 1-58017-026-9 (pbk.)
    1. Gardening. I. Title.
SB453.T496   1998

                                                    97-31826
                                                    CIP

Contents

Acknowledgments

The best part of writing this book was visiting the gardens of many green-thumb enthusiasts who have achieved some measure of "laziness" with their hobby and talking with others who shared their tips for more efficient gardening. I am indebted to: Marcia Barber, Ruth and Art Dewey, Closey Dickey, Kit and Tom Foster, Michael Hawks, Charles Hayward, Lesley Howell, Michael Jamieson, Deirdre Kevorkian, Joan Kevorkian, Bob and Eleanor Kolkebeck, Helen and Fabian Kunzelmann, Raymond Lambert, Kathy Link, Alice Moir, John Page, Marjorie Peff, Sally Robinson, Mary Sears, Ann Silverfarb, Nora Stevenson, Betty Vander Els, Philip Viereck, and Reg Young.

Getting started

WHO ARE "LAZY" GARDENERS? Most are busy people who neverthe-less want time in their lives for the feel of cool earth, the solace of planting, the joy of bloom, the satisfaction of producing food, and the taste of fresh picked. They want the most from their gardens with the least effort. Most of us are lazy gardeners.

The secret to leisurely gardening is good organization. If you tend a garden for the joy of it, you don't want to be a slave to it. Gardeners who are successfully lazy have planned effectively the layout of the garden, the choice of plants, and a schedule of seasonal jobs and regu-lar maintenance, which, timed properly, saves later grief. Five minutes now will save an hour in the future.

Get Organized!

First, decide what you want from your land. Whether you've lived with your landscape for years, have inherited a garden from previous owners, or are planning a new plot, take time to weigh your choices. Paradise is a garden, so when you create a garden make sure it is, for you, more paradise than punishment.

Although the primary focus of this book is vegetable gardening, some information on landscaping and flower gardening is included, in

A MASTER PLAN FOR THE PERFECT PLOT

Whether you are creating a general landscape plan or designing a flower bed or a vegetable garden, **lay it out on paper** first. Use tracing pads of graph paper, available at stores that sell engineering and drafting supplies; it comes in two sizes, 8½ by 11 inches or 11 by 17 inches. You can choose from several grid sizes, but **four squares to the inch** is most practical for laying out a garden to scale.

One advantage of this method is that you can overlay this year's vegetable garden on last year's to plan crop rotations easily. Note each vegetable variety in the layout and, after you plant, the date of planting. The plan will ensure proper spacing in the garden and will make it possible to calculate how much seed to purchase.

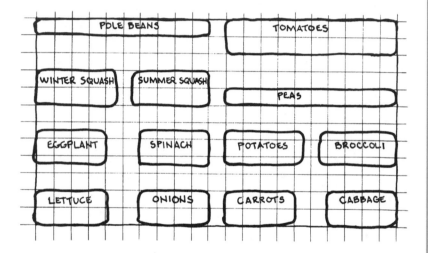

It is particularly important to plan flower gardens on paper if you interplant perennials and bulbs: you don't want to dig up bulbs after their foliage has ripened and disappeared. Use colored pencils to help visualize the color scheme.

One gardener keeps a blank sheet of tracing paper over her flower garden plan, and during the summer, as plants bloom, she indicates changes to be made. For instance:
- Move yarrow to back (it grew taller than expected).
- Trade places of coral bells and purple sage (for better color placement).

Plan the moves when color shows and do the moving at optimum time for planting.

the belief that as a wise lazy gardener you will maintain your entire yard and make changes that simplify your gardening chores.

As you think about those chores, ask yourself a few questions: How much time do you want to spend working the land? Do flowers give enough pleasure to justify their maintenance? Would you prefer to devote your limited time to growing only fruits and vegetables? How large a garden can you keep under control? Have your needs changed over the eras, and have you had the courage to change the garden?

In seeking answers, consult the experts and avoid costly or time-consuming mistakes. Use your Agricultural Extension Agent, a rich source of general gardening information, literature, and guidance. He or she can give you tips on what varieties of trees, shrubs, flowers, and vegetables grow well in your climate and soil type. Call the County Forester for information on recommended trees or advice on maintaining or improving those you already have. The Soil Conservation Service representative will tell you about local soils. A soil survey can be helpful in making decisions about land use. Some government personnel will even visit your land on request.

Time-Saving Routines

Keep a month-by-month **schedule of reminders** to make your work in the garden more efficient. In a looseleaf notebook, with a section for each month, list all the general jobs that need to be done, as well as the care particular plants require. The looseleaf format makes it simple to add or change information. For instance:

APRIL
General: work soil when possible.
Asparagus: Fertilize and cultivate.
Currants: Cover with nylon net.

"I just leave the notebook lying out in the kitchen. It saves time. Before I started this system, I was always flipping through books to find out what needed to be done. It was just so frustrating to remember what to do. This makes it so easy," explains an advocate of this method.

SEND A MESSAGE TO YOURSELF

How many times have you reached the garden, then remembered you forgot the ball of twine, the trowel? How many times have you promised yourself to make a note in your garden notebook — but forgotten it by the time you reached the house? Stop forgetting right now. Put up a post at one corner of your garden. Put a mailbox on it. The mail carrier won't deliver your gardening catalogs there, but you'll find it's a wonderful spot for trowels, twine, your notebook (don't forget a couple of pens or pencils), labels, pruning shears, a piece of worn sheeting from which to rip pieces to tie up the tomatoes — all those little things essential to gardening.

Stroll around your garden daily, shears or knife in hand. As you savor the sights, snip off dead blooms and pull out obvious weeds.

• • •

One gardener has divided her landscape into seven sections. "I never spend more than thirty minutes in any section," she says. "When the thirty minutes are up, I move on — either to another section or to the tennis court. I may spend only thirty minutes in the garden or a couple of hours, but everything receives some attention regularly, and I never feel behind."

The Ideal Site

Among other things, a vegetable garden needs:

- Day-long sun (at least eight hours)
- Good drainage (a slight slope to the south is ideal)
- Protection from cold wind

Keep it **away from trees** (their roots will steal nutrients from the garden) and as **near to the kitchen** as practicable. You'll take better care of a garden that is close to the house. You'll also spend more time there, gather crops more conveniently, and be on the lookout for garden problems and pests.

A Simple Layout

To **get maximum sun,** plant tallest crops on the north side of the garden, so they don't shade shorter ones, or make rows run north and south.

• • •

Lazy gardeners **locate frequently harvested crops closest to the house** to avoid compacting the soil by walking through the garden excessively.

WHAT YOU NEED, WHERE YOU NEED IT

Try a salad garden — perhaps a small raised bed — just outside the kitchen door. Plant ruby and green looseleaf lettuce, romaine, two pepper plants, two Pixie tomato plants, herbs such as basil (sweet and opal), chives, parsley (curly and Italian), and a few marigolds. Put a couple of stepping stones in the center. Often-used herbs are just a snip away, and the palette of greens and varied textures make a garden as eye-pleasing as any purely ornamental planting.

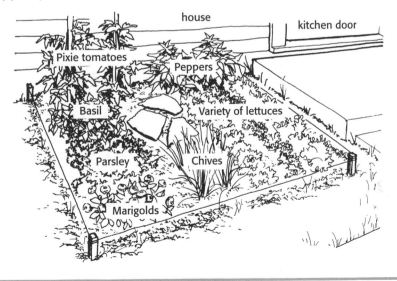

Plant vegetable families together in order to aid planning the rotation of crops in subsequent years:

- Legumes: peas, beans, limas
- Brassicas: cabbage, kale, broccoli, collards, cauliflowers, kohlrabi, Brussels sprouts
- Cucurbits: cucumber, melons, squash
- Nightshade family: peppers, tomatoes, potatoes, eggplant
- Root vegetables: beets, carrots, turnips, salsify, parsnips, radishes, rutabagas, onions, garlic, leeks
- Corn
- Leafy greens: spinach, chard, lettuce

If you are going to **cultivate with a rototiller,** make sure the rows are six to eight inches wider than the tiller itself.

• • •

Take advantage of all the space you have by utilizing vertical cropping, intercropping, and succession planting.

- Vertical cropping means training sprawling plants to grow up (see pages 47–56). Try it with cucumbers, squash, tomatoes, and melons.
- Intercropping means planting quick-maturing vegetables such as lettuce and spinach between widely spaced rows of a slow-maturing crop such as tomatoes, or growing squash in with corn.
- Succession planting means making a second planting, such as putting in beans where you've just harvested early spinach. Make sure to dig in compost or fertilizer before you replant.

Save Time, Save Space

Many gardeners are trying methods other than traditional, widely spaced rows of vegetables, methods that promise larger harvests with less work.

Widen Those Rows!

Instead of narrow rows one plant in width, broadcast seed in broad bands, anywhere from ten inches on up. A row the width of a rake is most practical. This planting method allows you to:

- Plant more quickly.
- Weed less (close planting leaves less space for weeds).
- Save watering, as the plants form a "living mulch" that shades the earth, traps dew for added moisture and counters drying of the soil by wind.
- Grow cool-weather crops such as spinach and lettuce in more heat because it won't bolt as fast in wide rows.
- Harvest more vegetables from less space.
- Reap a longer harvest from the same planting, since natural competitiveness of the closely spaced crop makes some plants mature earlier than others.

This system works well with most vegetables, but it can't be recommended for potatoes, tomatoes, corn, melons, squash, and cucumbers.

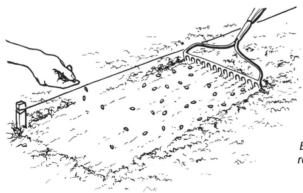

Broadcast seed in wide rows. A row the width of a rake is ideal.

Raise Those Beds!

In this system, vegetables are planted close together on beds that are ten inches wide or more and that are built up six to ten inches above ground level. Walkways run between the beds. Proponents claim higher yields from this method, four times more vegetables per acre than raised by commercial agriculture.

Rake smooth the top of a 6- to 10-inch high raised bed.

Advantages

- Drainage is improved.
- Soil warms faster, dries out more quickly in spring. That means you can plant earlier.
- Close planting leaves little room for weeds, and that means little or no weeding.
- Beds are small and all weeds are within easy reach.
- Plants provide a "living mulch," shading the soil and keeping it cooler.
- No one walks where plants are growing.
- Agony of digging deeply in rocky or shallow soils is avoided.
- Soil, continually enriched, becomes loose and friable.
- Beds can be formed in fall, to be ready for an early start where wet clay soils often delay planting.

Disadvantages

- Beds tend to dry out in summer heat.
- Paths between beds can become weedy.

To overcome these problems, peel thick "leaves" from bales of spoiled hay to cover the pathways. Add more hay if weeds sprout.

Sides of beds may be contained by pressure-treated lumber, if desired, but this isn't necessary. Indeed, the wooden sides may become a haven for snails. Beds can quickly be reshaped with a hoe or rake.

NOTE: When treating lumber or buying treated lumber, whether for raised beds or a back porch, use a copper-based preservative NOT a compound containing either pentachloro-phenol or creosote. These are toxic.

Retired friends of mine didn't want to bother with canning and freezing. They did, however, hanker for fresh tomatoes for the table and a few fresh vegetables. The only place with enough sun and away from roots of shade trees was smack in the middle of their back lawn. Two raised beds set side by side seemed to be the solution.

They rescued wooden pallets from the town dump, treated the lumber with copper naphthanate preservative, and used it to build sides for two beds four feet by nine feet. The lumber was set in trenches and extended eight inches above ground level. They mixed manure, compost, rock phosphate, sand, and peat moss with some topsoil to fill the beds. Their garden held three tomato plants, cucumbers, and squash — all trained inside wire cages — twin poles of Kentucky Wonder beans set at either end of one bed, carrots, a few broccoli and pepper plants, and a bit of leaf lettuce, with parsley, chives, and thyme planted around the edges. They decided it was best to concentrate on crops that keep producing rather than those that bear once and are finished. "It's extraordinary how many things we got in there," says the wife.

It's Okay to Be Square

In this method, the vegetable garden is laid out in sections four feet by four feet with paths between the squares. As with raised beds, you always walk in the paths, never in the beds. Seed spacing is figured by

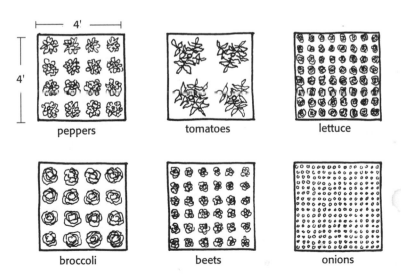

Plant in squares to yield more harvest from less land.

the number of seeds (or transplants) per square foot. A one-foot square of garden holds, for instance, one pepper plant or four heads of lettuce or nine beets or sixteen onions. Vining crops are trained vertically.

Advantages
- Soil is never compacted by foot traffic, because you can reach everything in the garden from the defined paths.
- You get more harvest from less land. You need much less space than you would for the same harvest planted in conventional rows.
- Less land in garden means less weeding, less watering, and less compost and other materials to enrich soil.
- Overplanting is avoided.
- Garden looks neater.
- No thinning is needed with the single-seed sowing method.
- Crop rotation is easy to figure and doesn't require elaborate planning.
- No power tools are needed once the garden is established.
- Soil is enriched bit by bit after each square foot is harvested, so no big spring soil preparation is necessary.

Disadvantages
- A system best suited to neat individuals.
- Slower planting in spring.

• • •

One gardener I know — a school principal — has combined elements of all three of the above layouts with wonderful results. He has raised beds three or four inches high, plants in rows four feet wide, and uses the broadcast method for small seeds and the square-foot method for larger seeds and transplants.

When I visited his garden, he explained why he chose this hybrid approach: "I must make good use of my time. Besides, the busiest times in the garden — May and September — are also the busiest times at school."

He gets his fifty-foot-square garden planted in one working day. "Essentially, all I do is plant and harvest," he says. "The rest takes care of itself."

Easy Landscaping

Unique Walks

Examine traffic patterns of people and pets before you decide where to put walks or to relocate existing ones. Use walks to direct foot traffic, to provide boundaries for flower or shrub borders, and to divide flower and vegetable gardens into sections, so that you never have to step in planting areas in order to seed, cultivate, or harvest. In the vegetable garden, raised beds and square beds incorporate walks into the garden plan. Flower gardeners warn, "Never have a wide perennial bed without paths into it, or maintenance is a struggle."

• • •

To **avoid weeding** walks, underlay paths with black plastic before covering with crushed stone, gravel, marble chips, crushed sea shells, shredded bark, wood chips, or crushed roofing tile.

• • •

In the vegetable garden, **mowed grass paths** look neat, are easy to care for and the separate beds they create help when planning crop rotation.

• • •

More elaborate walks are made of slate, flagstone, marble, bricks, broken-up concrete, or slices of cedar or old telephone poles surrounded by wood chips. Invest enough time and effort to make the project lasting and virtually care-free. Good drainage is essential. Put a six-inch layer of gravel, cinders, or sand under the paving material. In northern areas where ground freezes deeply, masonry walks may heave during the spring thaw. In these areas of the country, it is more practical to set everything in a bed of sand instead of using mortar.

Lawn and Tree Basics

Make an easy, low maintenance lawn by simply **not planting grass.** Just mow whatever happens to grow there. In a season or less a natural lawn will develop.

• • •

Repairing empty patches in lawns used to be a tedious job, but no more. Recently some garden supply catalogs have begun offering a lawn repair product most commonly called **turf mats.** The mat looks like a rug and is made from a biodegradable mulch laced with grass seed. To repair your lawn simply prepare the soil, cut the mat to fit the patch, and water twice a day until the grass begins to grow.

* * *

Keep lawns in **simple shapes** to eliminate maneuvering with the mower and hand trimming.

* * *

Don't scatter trees and shrubs in random fashion over the lawn. Not only will the mower go crazy dodging and swerving through this obstacle course, but a moment of inattention can mean a nick in the bark of a tree, an entry point for insect enemies and disease. Instead, **plant trees in groups,** forming islands in the lawn. Tie the space together and smother sod the easy way by applying a thick layer of newspapers or magazines and covering them with three or four inches of shredded bark or other good-looking mulch. The following season poke holes in the newspaper under the mulch (the sod will have decomposed) and plant drifts of daffodils or other bulbs.

* * *

A **ground cover** takes hold quickly in a mulched tree island and, once established, adds texture and eliminates the need to replenish the mulch. You might want to substitute ground covers for lawn in other places, where it is too shady for grasses to grow well or too steep to mow easily. Ground covers can also provide a transition from lawn to woods. Or simply plant ground cover to reduce the amount of lawn to be mowed. Ground covers for shady places are pachysandra, vinca minor, sweet woodruff, lily of the valley, European ginger, winter creeper, ivies, and ferns. In sun, try one of the creeping junipers, ajuga, heathers, or cotoneaster.

TRIMMING FOR TRADITIONALISTS

For the die-hard traditionalists who insist there are a few places that simply must be hand-trimmed, an old-fashioned, hand sheep shear is the tool to get, advises one of my meticulous gardening friends. "It's lightweight, sharp, and better than all the fancy gadgets on the market," she says. Buy one modified for garden use and sold as an "English garden shear."

When planning a tree island, flower garden, or planting bed, use rope or twine and experiment with possible boundaries before you commit to planting. A design on paper may look entirely different when actually planted, and you may need to adjust your proposed scheme several times before you discover exactly the right layout.

• • •

Avoid hedges. They need to be trimmed.

• • •

Choose hardy plant material, preferably grown (or acclimatized) in a local nursery, or at least one in your own gardening zone. The less the shock of transplanting, the more quickly it will begin to prosper. You may be tempted to bring in exotics, but if they are not comfortable in your environment, they will be susceptible to diseases, pests, and winterkill — all of which mean more work for you.

Edging – A Graceful Touch

Edging beds and gardens by hand can be a time-consuming, unrewarding chore. Time spent in installing permanent edging saves on regular maintenance:

- Bricks or paving blocks at or slightly lower than lawn level provide a mowing strip, eliminating the need for hand trimming.
- Pressure-treated lumber can be used to make raised beds that lawn will not invade.
- Commercial rubberlike (really polyethylene) edging with a rounded top can be shaped into curves for a free-form planting bed, then sunk into the earth so only the top lip shows. A flange on the bottom keeps it from popping up, and a steel spike driven in every four or five inches prevents frost heaving. Comes in black or brown. It keeps a pine bark mulch in and grass out of the bed.

Commercial polyethylene edging can minimize time needed for maintenance.

Easy Flower Gardens

If you border on woods, create a woodland garden as a **transition from lawn to forest.** Heavily mulch with shredded bark and plant under trees with shade-loving shrubs such as rhododendron, mountain laurel, and andromeda. Add color with easy-care spring bulbs and primroses. Summer bloom from impatiens and fibrous- and tuberous-rooted begonias complements ferns and ground covers such as wild ginger or pachysandra. I have friends who created a garden like this when they moved into a new house. They laid the heavy cardboard from their packing boxes on scythed weeds at wood's edge, piled wood chips on top, and waited a season before planting anything.

• • •

Instead of planning and planting flower beds, fill half barrels, crocks, or other large tubs with rich soil mix and plant with bright annuals. This **mobile color** can be placed wherever a perky accent is needed.

• • •

What about **perennial borders?** Don't they just come up every year without care?

"That's a popular fallacy about perennial beds," insists a devoted gardener. "People think they're not any work. That notion is for the birds. Once established, perennials are cheaper than annuals, because you don't have to buy new plants each year, but to have a successful perennial bed you must continually divide and replant. I use the English system of massing the border with plants so close together that weeds have no space to grow, but that means I must divide more frequently. And the work in the fall — cutting down all the top growth — phew!"

• • •

"I spend about an hour once a week in my perennial garden." says another flower enthusiast. "But every spring and fall there are times when I go at my garden for whole days, to dig up and replant."

• • •

Spring bulbs are beautiful to see in bloom, but achingly difficult to plant in the fall. Just think of how long it would take to dig holes for a few hundred crocus bulbs. A new tool, called a **bulb auger,** makes digging those holes a lot easier. The tool fits onto a standard electric hand drill and can dig up to 500 holes in an hour.

Herb-Growing Techniques

If you have a sunny spot, try an herb garden. Herbs have no special soil requirements except good drainage, are bug-free, and are among the easiest plants to grow. Perennials include bee balm, catnip, chives, lavender, mints, sage, tansy, tarragon, thymes, wormwood, and yarrow. Marjoram and rosemary are hardy only in warm climates. (Up north, plant them in tubs and use as houseplants in winter.) Feverfew, a biennial, reseeds itself, and you may want some annuals such as basil, borage, calendula, dill, nasturtium, and summer savory.

RESTRAINING MINT

To **keep mint from spreading** and becoming a nuisance, sink a chimney flue tile in the ground and plant inside its walls.

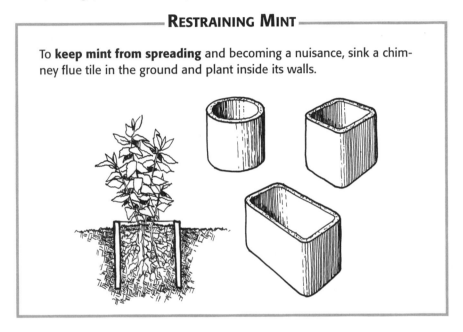

An herb enthusiast explains, "I grow herbs because I can use them in many ways, and I can have a messy garden without excuses." She has organized her **herbs in raised beds.** "It looks attractive even in winter," she adds. Each bed holds an assortment of herbs for a particular purpose: drying, tea, medicinal, and fragrance. She keeps culinary herbs just outside the kitchen door.

Pesto is one of the bounties of summer and you can have it fast and easy by planting a **thick carpet of basil** in the garden instead of planting the herb in neat rows. As the basil sprouts simply wait until it is a few inches high and harvest it all.

Six Tool Tips

1. Sometimes the labels placed at the heads of garden rows fade in the summer sun until they are unreadable. No matter what type of label you use mark them with a **weatherproof garden or laundry pen** and the writing will be clear and crisp for many seasons. The pens are usually less than $3.00 each and will save you much aggravation and time.

2. Hand pruning can make finger joints and hands sore in no time. To relieve some of the discomfort switch to **ergonomically designed pruners.** Instead of the traditional straight handle of most pruners, the new style featured by companies such as Felco and Sandvik have curved handles that make using them much more enjoyable.

3. Every few years there seems to be a **new hoe design** touted to be better than its ancestors. In the end the easiest, most efficient hoes to use are the stirrup hoes, the strange looking swoe, and the colinear hoe. Each of these allows fast, easy uprooting of weeds while cultivating the soil.

4. Bending over for hours on end while planting the garden can be fatiguing at best. Traditional dibbles made holes for seeds faster than other methods, but they were so short that bending over to make the holes was still unavoidable. A **walking stick with a brass end** makes a nice garden dibble that allows you to make seed holes all day and never bend over once.

5. Lots of people have an outdoor thermometer in the garden that serves more for decoration than practical use. Switch that old decorative one for a **max-min thermometer** which will allow you to gauge the climate conditions in the garden much more accurately.

6. Of the many ways to easily water the garden and save water at the same time perhaps no product is better than the **soaker hose.** Also called a weeping hose, this hose allows water to leak uniformly at the rate of about one gallon per minute per fifty feet of hose. It can be installed above or below ground and under mulch and uses up to 70 percent less water than conventional watering systems.

Build the Soil

LAZY GARDENERS KNOW that if you tend to your soil, the tending of your crops will require less time. Make yourself a promise: never plant anything — tree, shrub, plant, or seed — unless you have first replenished the soil's organic matter in some way.

Organic matter improves the physical condition of the soil and increases the availability of nutrients to plants.

Whether your soil is clay, sand, or loam, adding organic matter will improve the way its particles cluster together. Clay is composed of tiny flakes that stick to each other and make clay soil difficult to work, for both the gardener and the soil microorganisms. When wet, it is mucky; when dry, it's like cement. Organic matter helps to bind small particles of clay in aggregates, so that a crumbly structure is formed, with spaces for air. In a sandy soil, organic matter helps to hold moisture and nutrients longer.

It is amazing to think that 25 percent of "good" soil is air and 25 percent water. Organic matter forms only 1 to 5 percent of the soil and the rest is mineral matter. Ironically, all those minerals sitting there are often unavailable to plants. Organic matter can make the minerals available.

A plant can't use raw organic matter. It waits until that matter has been broken down with the help of earthworms and microorganisms, into its basic elements. Humic acid is one product of decomposition, and it helps to make the soil's locked-up minerals, especially phosphorus and iron, available to plants. Practically all nitrogen in the soil comes from decomposing organic matter, which releases ammonia, a nitrogen compound. All this may seem complicated, but nature takes care of it easily. In the forest, when leaves fall to the forest floor, the tree returns to earth the nourishment that will fuel a new spring's growth. We can take a cue from nature and try to return to the soil at least as much as our crops take from it.

Good soil prevents many ills. It gives plants the opportunity for vigorous growth. You can't have vigorous top growth without vigorous root growth, and you can't have root growth without an aerated soil. Organic matter helps to aerate the soil; it also holds moisture and encourages the population of worms and beneficial bacteria.

Healthy plants resist disease and insect attack. Just as carnivorous predators attack the weak of the herd, insects go after weak plants. Healthy plants grow larger and shade out weeds sooner. Weeds come out of a loose, friable soil more easily than from trampled hardpan.

So build a healthy soil for healthy plants. Water less, weed less, fight fewer pests, and reap more bountiful harvests.

All-Purpose Cover Crops

Green manures (also called cover crops) will improve soil quality. A green manure crop is plowed under right in place, adding organic matter high in nitrogen to the soil. In decomposing, it produces humic acid, which helps release locked-up minerals, so you need to add less fertilizer in other forms. A green manure crop also prevents erosion and crowds out weeds. Its root system helps loosen subsoil and bring up minerals. It improves soil structure in the same way that compost does, without the hauling — a boon to the lazy gardener.

Cover crops can be a solution for a gardener who wants to be lazier but can't bear to cut down on the size of the garden. Each year, plant half the space in a green manure and the other half in vegetables. The next season, switch places. You'll have half the work, eliminate many weeds, and be lazily improving your soil at the same time.

PLANT IN SPRING AND HARVEST OR TURN UNDER SAME SEASON:

Legumes: snap beans, soy beans, peas
Non-legumes: buckwheat, pearl millet, Sudan grass

In the South
Legumes: cowpeas, hairy indigo, espedeza, soy beans

PLANT IN SPRING AND HARVEST FOLLOWING SPRING:

Legumes: alfalfa, clovers (alsike, red, white), sweet clovers (white, yellow)

PLANT IN LATE SUMMER/EARLY FALL AND HARVEST OR TURN UNDER FOLLOWING SPRING:

Legume: hairy vetch
Non-legumes: barley, bromegrass, kale, oats, winter rye, annual ryegrass, wheat

In the South
Legumes: clovers (bur, crimson), lupines, vetches

Other "double-duty" crops you can harvest first, then turn under as green manure, are **soy beans** (and, in the South, cowpeas) and **kale.** Plant kale six weeks before first frost in the North or as a winter crop in the South.

• • •

Plant a cover crop of clover or another legume **between rows of corn.** Eliminate the need to weed and have soil replenishment for this heavy feeder ready and waiting.

• • •

My neighbor plants **winter rye** in his garden, section by section, as the seasons's last crops are harvested. A "piecework" approach keeps it from becoming a major project. Here in the Northeast, all the winter rye must be sown by October 15, when the growing season slows down, or it won't have a chance to become established before winter.

Legumes such as peas and beans make a valuable addition to the soil, because they have the ability to "fix" nitrogen: take it from the air and bind it to their roots. After the crop has been harvested, merely use a spade or tiller to turn the plants under, right then and there, where they will quickly decompose — green manuring in its simplest form.

Pull a bean plant and examine its root system. You can see the little nodules where the nitrogen-fixing bacteria hang out.

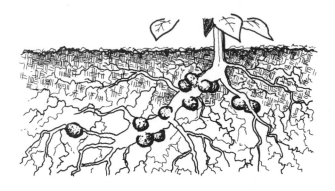

In spring, he spreads manure on top of the rye (optional) and plows both under. If desired, you can cut or disk the rye first.

• • •

Annual ryegrass dies out during the winter, so it is easier to turn under in spring than crops that survive.

• • •

Always **plow under a green manure before it goes to seed.** You don't want to have your soil improver become a weed in the vegetable crop that follows it.

Compost: The Essential Ingredient

Lazy gardeners argue about compost. Some insist nothing can take the place of a shovelful of compost mixed in planting holes for tomatoes, peppers, eggplant, and members of the cabbage family. Melons, cucumbers, and squash need its richness to send out strong, healthy vines. Use compost to side-dress hungry crops, mix it into the seedbed, or cover fine seeds with it as you plant, they say. Feed your vegetables and flowers with compost, and sit back and watch them grow.

Followers of Ruth Stout, author of *How to Have a Green Thumb Without an Aching Back* and *Gardening Without Work*, scoff at conventional composting schemes. "Why spend all that time carting stuff around?" they ask. They keep a thick mulch of hay on their gardens year-round, tuck kitchen waste under the hay, and toss all other organic materials on top. "Let them rot where the plants need them," they say.

No-Nonsense Composting

If you're a purist, you'll follow Sir Albert Howard's lead. He invented **the Indore method,** which calls for building a series of layers with a three-to-one ratio of green matter to manure:

1. Six inches of green matter (weeds, leaves, etc.)
2. Two inches of manure, garbage, or other high-nitrogen source
3. A sprinkling of soil (plus ground limestone and ground phosphate rock)

Repeat layers until the pile is four or five feet high. Moisten each layer as you build the pile so it is about as wet as a squeezed-out sponge. Poke holes in it with a rod to aid aeration. Turn the pile in six weeks and use it after three months.

Most of us aren't that organized. We want to recycle biodegradable waste, but we want to do it lazily.

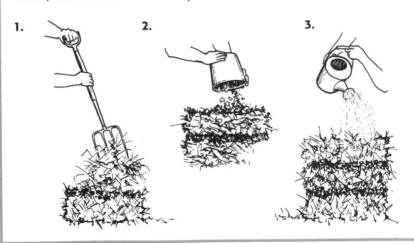

1.   2.   3.

"Composting is no bother at all, once you've established a system," counter its advocates.

Read too much about compost, and you'll be scared off completely. Carbon-nitrogen ratios, aeration, exact proportions of ingredients, activators, psychrophles, mesophiles, termophiles — help!

Despite all the hocus-pocus, compost is basically decomposed plant material; it looks like black, fluffy soil. Whether you make it in place as year-round mulch or in a separate bin doesn't matter. Once you've tried compost, never again will you be able to stand looking at crusty, dried-out soil of little tilth.

• • •

Keep a half-gallon milk carton or similar container next to the kitchen sink. Form the habit of filling it with the **kitchen's vegetable waste:** parings, eggshells, fruit pits and rinds, coffee grounds, tea

A THREE-BIN SYSTEM

Organic gardener Sam Ogden, author of *Organic Vegetable Growing*, is also an advocate of the powers of time. He uses three side-by-side bins for compost, each about five feet by twelve feet. One bin holds finished compost, one holds last year's slowly rotting compost pile, and the third is for this season's accumulation of kitchen garbage, weeds, spent pea vines, and other garden trash. He covers each layer of green matter (thin layers for better aeration) with a thin layer of soil. Rain provides moisture, and in two years the finished compost is fine, dark, and crumbly. Once this system is working, you'll always have one bin to draw from, so it's rather like an asparagus bed — two years of expectation and from then on the harvest keeps coming.

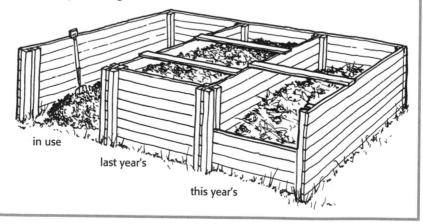

in use

last year's

this year's

leaves, carrot tops, cabbage cores, etc. When it is full, toss its contents on the compost pile.

. . .

"We have a great pile of compost, more than we'll ever use," says my neighbor. "What's the use of going through all that fuss — layering, proportioning, turning? Just throw all your weeds, leaves, clippings, and kitchen-vegetable waste in a pile and **let time do it** all."

. . .

"You can work at compost as if you're cooking a wonderful French ragout," says a gardener who savors her product. "Try to make it as interesting and diverse as possible."

. . .

If you can't wait two years for the three-bin system to mature and you don't want to scavenge, here are three ways to **speed up decomposition** of compost:

- Increase the ratio of **nitrogen** to carbon in the compost pile. Materials high in carbon include wood shavings, sawdust, dry leaves, and straw. Materials high in nitrogen are fresh grass clippings, fresh manure, vegetable wastes, green vegetation, and fertilizers such as blood meal, fish meal or alfalfa meal. Don't get *too* much nitrogen or you'll end up with slime.
- Increase the amount of **air** in the pile by laying perforated pipe at intervals as you build the pile. Every foot or so in height lay a few pipes horizontally a foot or two apart.
- Increase the **surface area** of ingredients by shredding them with a shredder or rotary mower before heaping. (If you want to bother moistening and turning the pile after four, seven, and ten days, you can have finished compost in two weeks.)

The **French Intensive Method** does not advocate the use of manures or rock powders in compost. It's simpler, they think, to make compost with three layers:

- One-third vegetation
- One-third kitchen waste
- One-third soil

COMPOSTING MATERIALS

Materials for composting and soil enrichment can be limited to those you generate yourself. If you have imagination and the initiative to scavenge a bit, figuring the time spent in building your soil will mean lush crops that grow with less of your midsummer energy, here's a list of possibilities:

apple pomace (by-product of cider-making)

bird-cage cleanings

brewery wastes

buckwheat hulls

cannery wastes

castor bean pomace

chaff

cheese whey

cocoa bean hulls

corn cobs and husks

cottonseed hulls and gin trash

dust from vacuum cleaner

evergreen needles

feathers

felt waste

fish scraps

garden residues (spent plants and vines, beet and carrot tops, corn stalks, etc.)

gelatin-processing waste

grape pomace (by-product of winemaking)

grass clippings

hair

hay

kitchen wastes (vegetable and fruit rinds, parings, egg shells, coffee grounds, tea leaves, etc.)

leather waste and dust

leaves

manures (horse, cow, goat, pig, rabbit, poultry)

milk, sour

mill wastes of lignin, wool, silk, and felt

nut shells

oat hulls

olive residues

peanut hulls

peat and sphagnum moss

pine needles

pond weeds

rice hulls

salt hay

sawdust and shredded bark

seaweed, kelp, eelgrass

straw

sugar cane

tanbark

tobacco stems and dust

woodchips and rotted wood

The minimum size for proper heating up of a compost pile is three feet by three feet by three feet. **Heat speeds decomposition** and kills disease-causing organisms and weed seeds.

Composters Beware!

- **Sewage sludge** may contain heavy metals.
- Don't put bones and other **animal wastes** in the compost pile. They do not decompose quickly and may invite animals to raid the pile.

Chicken manure is so strong we are warned about the danger of its burning crops. Sawdust has such a high carbon content we are told to add it sparingly to compost piles and never to put it on the garden without first giving plants a "booster" feeding of nitrogen. Sawdust and chicken manure are an ideal combination. The acidity of the sawdust offsets the alkalinity of the chicken manure.

NATURAL FERTILIZERS

Finely textured materials may be added directly to soil rather than to the compost pile, although the high-nitrogen ones act as activators to speed decomposition.

HIGH IN NITROGEN

alfalfa meal
blood meal and dried blood
horn and hoof meal
cottonseed meal (slightly acid)
linseed meal
soybean meal
fish meal

HIGH IN PHOSPHORUS

bone meal
rock phosphate

HIGH IN POTASSIUM

wood ashes
greensand (marl)
granite and marble dust

TO RAISE pH OF SOIL

limestone
Dolomitic limestone (also contains calcium and magnesium)

The Convenient Compost Pile

Where you put your compost pile will influence your attitude toward it. Think of it as an easy way to dispose of waste you have to get rid of anyhow. It should be near, or even in, your garden. The less hauling you have to do, the more convenient it will be to stockpile and use.

If you are a scavenger who collects composting materials from other places, try to locate your pile somewhere near your driveway, as well.

Good drainage is important, so too are proximity to a water supply if you live in a dry climate and some shelter from wind.

Sensible Containers

It's a good idea to **contain your compost pile** in some way. You can get plans for compost bins that would need a contractor to build. Or you can do it the easy way.

I have a lazy gardening friend who has spotted a few "retired" tomato cages (see pages 47–56) strategically around her garden as compost makers. She never has to walk far to deposit weeds or spent plants. When she needs a bit of compost to put under tomato, eggplant, or pepper transplants, it's right there. Scarlet runner beans or peas often may be found climbing the outside of the cages, camouflaging their contents.

* * *

Build two bins side by side, one for adding to, one for taking from.

* * *

Build a bin with **bales of hay.** The hay itself will eventually decompose. Then you can either add it to the pile and replace it with fresh bales, or toss it on your garden as mulch or to be tilled in, depending on the time of year.

* * *

If you have limited space, you can compost in a **garbage can** or drum. Punch holes in the bottom and sides (for drainage and aeration), set on bricks or concrete blocks, and layer materials with soil inside.

Commercial compost containers are also available. Most are designed so the finished compost can be removed through an opening near the bottom. They are quite expensive, however.

Toss garden wastes, table scraps, lawn clippings, leaves, and anything else that can be composted into a black **plastic bag** lining a trash can. When the can is filled, add a quart or two of water — enough to have everything moist but with no excess water. Tie the bag, then dump it out of the can and into a shaded spot. Start another bag. This is anaerobic (without oxygen) composting, so until the materials are completely rotted, they'll have the breathtaking smell of a septic tank, rather than the clean, woodsy smell of an aerobic compost pile.

• • •

Gerald Smith of the University of Georgia College of Agriculture, suggests this work-free method of composting leaves, which works fine in his mild winter season:

Rake **leaves** into plastic bags. Carry them to an inconspicuous and shaded area where they can be stored. Add enough water to each bag to wet the leaves thoroughly. Turn the bags over several times to wet down all of the leaves, then pour out any extra water. Gerald says, "Broadleaf leaves such as oak, maple, and pecan, collected in the fall, should be decomposed enough to work into the soil by April or May."

EASY COMPOSTING

For a simple system, get a piece of **sturdy wire mesh,** about four or five feet high, and nine feet long. Wire the two ends together, forming a cylinder. Place it at a convenient location — where you'll be using the compost when it's ready. Fill it with weeds, the zucchini that's outdone itself, a shovelful of soil, then more garden or kitchen wastes. If you feel compelled to turn it, you can simply unhook the cylinder, move it adjacent to the pile, and fork the contents back in. Otherwise, just let it sit and lift or unhook the cylinder when decomposition is complete.

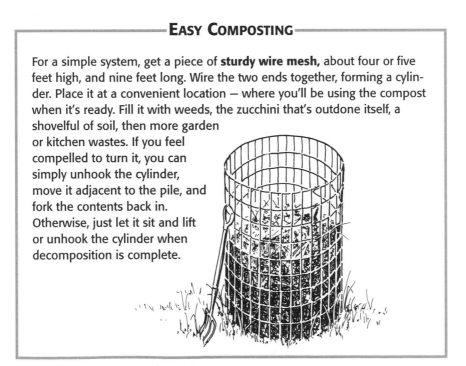

Compost Without a Pile

Do you plan to purchase **a new shrub or tree**? The summer or fall prior to planting, dig the hole. Dig it bigger than you think it needs to be. Layer it with composting materials and soil, building a small compost pit. Mulch lightly. In spring, the hard work of digging is behind you, for the friable soil that now fills the hole will come out ever so easily and be rich and ready to feed your new tree or shrub.

• • •

Make **compost for fruit trees** right under the trees. Leave a space three feet from the trunk, then layer materials for composting from there out to one foot beyond the drip line, about two feet high. The "doughnut" will feed the tree as it decomposes and do double duty as a mulch.

COMPOST IN CONCRETE

A three-sided **concrete-block bin** is easy to construct. Lay the block sideways (no mortar), and the holes will help let air in and gases out of the pile. If you want to get fancy, suspend perforated pipe at intervals between the holes in the blocks to promote even better aeration.

Or, lift the pile off the ground with pipes thrust between the second layer of blocks. Place wire mesh on the pipes. Evergreen branches laid on the wire will prevent most of the compost from sifting through the mesh. Build from there with composting materials. No turning is necessary, because of the ten-inch air space under the pile.

COMPOSTING METHODS

Try **strip composting.** Heap organic matter and manure on top of vegetable rows from which early crops have been harvested. The next season simply leave the composted material where it is, and at intervals scoop out a small hole for a shovelful of soil. Plant squash or cucumbers, or other heavy feeders, such as cabbage.

Or use the **two-hole method.** Make one hole between rows in your vegetable garden. Put the dirt aside. Dump the contents of your kitchen-waste container into the first hole. Cover it with dirt obtained by digging a second hole adjacent to the first. Now you have a hole ready for the next time you accumulate a container of parings. To cover it, dig a third hole, and the system continues.

Sheet composting eliminates carting. Spread leaves, manure, grass clippings, weeds, spent plants, and kitchen wastes directly on the soil and till them in. In cold climates, this is a wonderful fall project which disposes of all the leaves that bury lawns. Run a rotary mower over the leaves first and they'll decompose more quickly after they are turned under.

Lighten Clay Soil

There's no easy way to convert heavy clay to rich loam. There are ways that are hard work that don't work, and ways that are hard work that do work. In Georgia (and they know what heavy clay is in Georgia) Paul Colditz of the University of Georgia College of Agriculture says there's just one way to do it, "Add organic matter in large amounts."

A thin layer won't do it, he warns. It won't make a bit of difference. "Spread organic matter at least two inches thick over the soil and work it in to a depth of four to six inches. If peat moss is used, add limestone at a rate of five pounds per 100 square feet. If raw sawdust is added, extra nitrogen should be applied to feed the bacteria that break down this organic material. Broadcast one pound of nitrogen per ten square feet."

Other organic materials, such as compost or rotted leaves, can also be used. It takes a lot, as the accompanying table shows.

ORGANIC MATERIAL NEEDED
(TO COVER 100 SQUARE FEET)

DEPTH (INCHES)	AMOUNT OF ORGANIC MATTER
6	2 cubic yards
4	35 cubic feet
3	1 cubic yard
2	18 cubic feet
1	9 cubic feet

(1 cubic yard equals 27 cubic feet)

If you want to improve the texture of your soil quickly, buy **peat moss** or coarse **vermiculite** in large commercial bales (four cubic feet). Find a nursery or wholesaler to buy from.

Some gardeners with clay soil **add gypsum** at the rate of 20 pounds per 1000 square feet. It breaks up the soil more effectively than sand and keeps it from packing.

Soil Chemistry Made Simple

Sometimes a plant's poor performance results from the wrong pH. Test your soil to determine its degree of acidity or alkalinity. Your County Agent can tell you how to send soil to the state university for testing, or you can buy a home test kit. Do this in the fall. There's less waiting then, since soil labs are not as busy. If the test indicates that lime is needed, applying it in the fall means the soil and lime have time to react before spring planting.

• • •

Some plants that like sweet soils:
    alfalfa, clover, asparagus, brassicas, legumes, cucurbits,
    beets, chard, clematis, lilacs, iris
Some plants that like acid soils:
    watermelon, blueberries, strawberries, potatoes,
    broad-leaved evergreens

• • •

Potatoes must have either acid or very alkaline soil. If the soil is acid (below a pH of 5) or alkaline (above a pH of 7.5) then they are fine. Otherwise, they get scab. In the East, it's easier to make sure the soil is acid. In Idaho, the alkaline soil gives the characteristic dry, mealy quality to that state's famous potatoes.

• • •

To **make soil more acid,** add elemental sulfur (one-third pound per twenty-five square feet to lower pH one unit).

To **make soil more alkaline,** add lime (one pound per twenty-five square feet to raise pH one unit). Wood ashes also increase the alkalinity of soil. Use half the amount.

pH Preferences of Some Common Crops

Alfalfa	6.0–8.0	Garlic	5.5–8.0
Apple	5.0–6.5	Gooseberry	5.0–6.5
Artichoke (Jerusalem)	6.5–7.5	Grape	5.5–7.0
Asparagus	6.0–8.0	Grapefruit	6.0–7.5
Avocado	6.0–8.0	Hazelnut	6.0–7.0
Barley	6.5–7.8	Hickory nut	6.0–7.0
Bean, lima	6.0–7.0	Horseradish	6.0–7.0
Bean, pole	6.0–7.5	Kale	6.0–7.5
Beet, sugar	6.5–8.0	Kohlrabi	6.0–7.5
Beet, table	6.0–7.5	Kumquat	5.5–6.5
Blackberry	5.0–6.0	Leek	6.0–8.0
Blueberry	4.0–5.5	Lemon	6.0–7.0
Broccoli	6.0–7.0	Lentil	5.5–7.0
Broom sedge	4.5–6.0	Lespedeza	4.5–6.5
Brussels sprout	6.0–7.5	Lettuce	6.0–7.0
Buckwheat	5.5–7.0	Millet	5.0–6.5
Cabbage	6.0–7.5	Mushroom	6.5–7.5
Cantaloupe	6.0–7.5	Mustard	6.0–7.5
Carrot	5.5–7.0	Oats	5.0–7.5
Cashew	5.0–6.0	Okra	6.0–7.5
Cauliflower	5.5–7.5	Olive	5.5–6.5
Celery	5.8–7.0	Onion	6.0–7.0
Cherry, sour	6.0–7.0	Orange	6.0–7.5
Cherry, sweet	6.0–7.5	Parsley	5.0–7.0
Chicory	5.0–6.5	Parsnip	5.5–7.0
Chives	6.0–7.0	Pea	6.0–7.5
Clover, red	6.0–7.5	Peach	6.0–7.5
Corn	5.5–7.5	Peanut	5.3–6.6
Cotton, upland	5.0–6.0	Pear	6.0–7.5
Cowpea	5.0–6.5	Pecan	6.4–8.0
Crabapple	6.0–7.5	Pepper	5.5–7.0
Cranberry	4.2–5.0	Pineapple	5.0–6.0
Cucumber	5.5–7.0	Plum	6.0–8.0
Currant, red	5.5–7.0	Potato	4.8–6.5
Eggplant	5.5–6.5	Potato, sweet	5.2–6.0
Endive	5.8–7.0	Pumpkin	5.5–7.5

Quince	6.0–7.5	Squash, Hubbard	5.5–7.0
Radish	6.0–7.0	Strawberry	5.0–6.5
Raspberry, black	5.0–6.5	Swiss chard	6.0–7.5
Raspberry, red	5.5–7.0	Thyme	5.5–7.0
Rhubarb	5.5–7.0	Timothy	5.5–6.5
Rutabaga	5.5–7.0	Tomato	5.5–7.5
Sage	5.5–6.5	Turnip	5.5–6.8
Salsify	6.0–7.5	Vetch	5.2–7.0
Shallot	5.5–7.0	Walnut	6.0–8.0
Sorghum	5.5–7.5	Watercress	6.0–8.0
Soybean	6.0–7.0	Watermelon	5.5–6.5
Spinach	6.0–7.5	Wheat	5.5–7.5
Squash, crookneck	6.0–7.5		

Courtesy of Sudbury Laboratories, Inc.

You know that **ashes** from the fireplace are fine for the garden, but you're not about to trudge through the snow to scatter them there. So you dump them in a cardboard box and put it in the garage. That spells TROUBLE. If there's a single ember in those ashes, it's likely to set the cardboard afire. Use a metal can — a trash can is fine — for wood ashes. It will keep them dry until you scatter them in the spring. Limit the ashes to one or two ten-quart pails to 1,000 square feet each year.

• • •

Have fun with **hydrangea color** by controlling the pH of the soil. Acid soil (a pH of 4.5 to 5.5) produces blue flowers. Alkaline soil (a pH of 7 to 7.5) gives pink ones.

11 Special Tips

1. **Azaleas** love left-over tea and tea leaves. So do houseplants such as philodendron and rubber plants.

2. Spread a thick layer of manure on the **asparagus patch** after the ground freezes in fall. It does double duty as winter protection and an early source of nutrients in spring.

3. A Long Island gardener smiles mischievously when you marvel at the size and beauty of his **glorious roses.** "Just don't try to walk through that bed," warns his son. "It squishes." His secret? He visits fishing party boats as they return from salt water outings, and they gladly give him the entrails of fish caught and cleaned by paying customers. Area fish markets are equally obliging. He buries his scavenged treasure among the roses, and they thank him with giant blooms.

4. Fill a shaker with **borax** and sprinkle on soil next to beets (provides boron).

5. To **provide magnesium** for faster development of tomatoes, peppers, and eggplants, mix two tablespoons Epsom salts to one gallon of water. Apply one pint to each plant just as bloom begins.

6. Mix one-half cup **Epsom salts** to one-half bushel wood ashes. Sprinkle around daffodils as they emerge from soil in spring. Adds potash, lime, magnesium.

7. Crushed egg shells mixed into soil around brassicas (cabbage, broccoli, cauliflower, etc.) provide **extra calcium,** which they need.

8. Sprinkle **coffee grounds** over carrot plantings to repel the root maggot or around evergreens as an eye-pleasing mulch.

9. Most plants benefit from receiving regular fertilizer applications, a process that can be messy and always takes time. To make fertilizing easy try using a **time-release fertilizer** such as Osmocote. The fertilizer is contained in small granules that slowly release their nutrients over many weeks and even months.

10. **Hold back** on nitrogen-rich fertilizer late in the season. Overly rich growth makes plants more susceptible to frost.

11. **Herbs like lime** and gritty soil. If you live in an area where ground oyster shells are available, mix one handful into each planting hole for herbs.

When the North Wind Blows

AH, WINTER! The fun begins. You pore over seed catalogs, read of new varieties. If you were smart, you made a list in fall of all the things that did or didn't work last year. Your plans are more practical when you can still remember that the watermelons were hit by frost before they ripened than when the promises of seed catalogs cloud your vision.

Assess the successes and failures of last year's garden. Did you grow what your family likes to eat? No sense nurturing cauliflower if no one will touch it. Did you keep up with the zucchini harvest? Maybe you need only one or two hills this year. Or forget it entirely. Your neighbor will love you for giving him an outlet for his surplus, and you'll have more space for other crops. Are you using all your garden space productively? Perhaps you'll decide to plant in wide rows or square beds this year. Will you put part of your plot in a cover crop, or grow more flowers or a space-user like corn, for which you never had room with your old system? Or is it time to reduce the size of your garden permanently, now that your children have grown up and moved on?

Be realistic. Decide which crops you truly want to grow, and in what quantity. Do you need just enough to eat fresh, or do you want a surplus to freeze, can, or dry? Lay out your garden on paper and order only enough seed to match your plan. Choose disease-resistant strains. Talk to your gardening friends about varieties that have performed well in their gardens. Follow the experts in choosing a new variety. Try an All-America Selection winner; new ones are selected each year by a non-profit organization of seedsmen.

Get as much done as you can before planting time arrives. Winter is not only for planning, it's for organizing and repairing tools, for preparing staking systems (if you use them), for lettering markers to be placed in your garden at planting, for ordering hardware for fencing — a gathering of momentum so you are all ready for the joy of placing that first seed in moist earth.

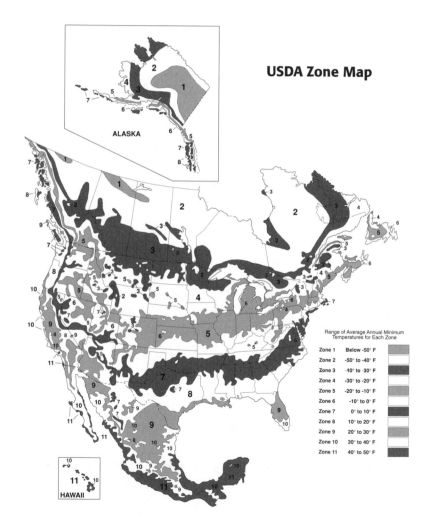

USDA Zone Map

Range of Average Annual Minimum Temperatures for Each Zone

Zone 1	Below -50° F
Zone 2	-50° to -40° F
Zone 3	-40° to -30° F
Zone 4	-30° to -20° F
Zone 5	-20° to -10° F
Zone 6	-10° to 0° F
Zone 7	0° to 10° F
Zone 8	10° to 20° F
Zone 9	20° to 30° F
Zone 10	30° to 40° F
Zone 11	40° to 50° F

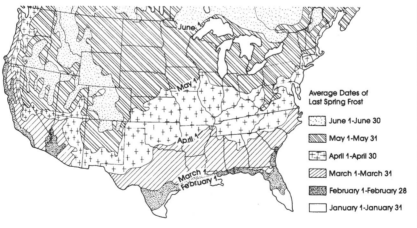

Average Dates of
First Fall Frosts

- July 1-July 31
- August 1-August 31
- September 1-September 30
- October 1-October 31
- November 1-November 30
- December 1-December 31

Average Dates of
Last Spring Frost

- June 1-June 30
- May 1-May 31
- April 1-April 30
- March 1-March 31
- February 1-February 28
- January 1-January 31

You can time your seed sowing, transplanting, and fall-season crops by estimating the average dates of the last frost in spring and first frost in fall in your area.

All About Seeds

Half-used packages of seed lie before you. Will you take a chance and plant them next year? What if few germinate? That would be a waste of time and energy. You can throw the old seeds away and start with fresh packets each spring, or you can test the leftovers to find out which batches are still viable.

Dampen a paper towel. Lay ten seeds of the same variety on it. Cover with another damp paper towel. To provide continuous moisture, either mist occasionally with water or roll the towel gently and place it in a plastic bag. Label it and put it in a warm place, next to rising yeast dough, perhaps. After the germination time has elapsed (find it on the package) count the number of seeds that have sprouted. Seven or eight is a good number. If fewer than 50 percent have germinated, order new seed.

Try the same experiment in a petri dish, the covered plastic disc scientists use for growing cultures. Put a moistened paper towel, tissue, or damp cotton in the bottom, then lay out the ten seeds and replace the cover. Watch the progress of germination without disturbing the seeds. Radish root hairs are amazing! Keep a magnifying glass nearby to enjoy the show.

• • •

Store seeds in a cool, dry place. Keep them in a metal canister in a cool cabinet, or place them in a covered glass jar in the refrigerator, with a package of desiccant as a companion.

• • •

When seeds arrive, **sort and file** them by planting season — early, middle, and late. Be ready for the blind rush to the garden in spring.

• • •

Not all seeds are created equal; some are bigger than others of their kind. A trick to get bigger plants that bear faster and larger yields is to **separate seeds by size.** The largest seeds will generally bear earlier, larger crops.

• • •

Ray Lambert declares that buying from seed catalogs is the downfall of the over-extended gardener. "It's too tempting to buy more than you need or have space to grow," he explains. "I buy seed in bulk at the local feed store — only once and only what I need. The total cost of everything for my fifty-by-fifty-foot garden this year was twenty-five dollars, including transplants."

. . .

"I save the most money by growing asparagus," states Phil Viereck. "I harvest fifty to seventy-five dollars worth of tender spears from my bed each year."

Transplanting Vegetables

Some vegetables just hate to be transplanted and produce better crops when direct sown. Save indoor space and transplanting time by planting squash, pumpkin, melons, and cucumbers directly in the garden after the soil warms in spring.

In the Tool Shed

During the winter, end summer's frantic rummaging. **Organize your tools.** If each one has its own hook, you will never waste time searching for it. Pegboard provides a flexible method of storing tools, since you can move hooks around to accommodate new purchases.

. . .

Clean metal parts of spades, shovels, forks, rakes, and hoes with a wire brush, emery cloth, or steel wool. Apply a protective coating of oil with an old cloth. Floor wax will rejuvenate the handles.

Then set up a **time-saver** for next season. Fill an old pail with sand. Pour into it a quart or so of oil (used motor oil is fine), and mix it a bit. After every use of your hoes, rakes, shovels, and other hand tools, push them into the oily sand a few times. They'll emerge shiny and with a film of oil to keep them from rusting. They'll last a lot longer, and you'll never again have the dreary job of polishing rust off them.

. . .

Attach an old rake head to the wall and use it as a **hanger for hand tools.**

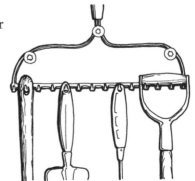

Rake-head tool hanger

Your garden shouldn't be shaded — but there should be some shade nearby — and this bench should be in it. Build it in two hours, and enjoy it on those warm afternoons when the weeds won't grow much anyway.

You need an 8-foot 2" x 12" (or wider) for the seat and legs, and a 4-foot 2" x 4" for a brace. Cut two 14-inch pieces from the plank for legs, leaving a seat area 68 inches long. Center the 2" x 4" brace between the legs, glue with exterior-type glue, and attach with ½" x 4" countersunk flat-head wood screws. Attach legs to seat by gluing and using same size screws. Finish as you please.

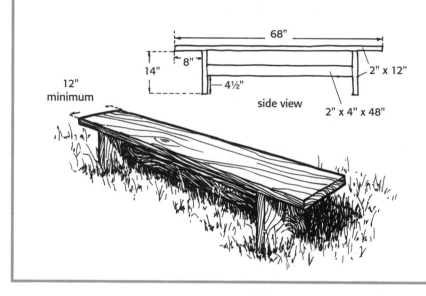

Paint a band of red, orange, or yellow on the handles of all your tools. Makes them easier to find when you inadvertently dump them into the compost pile along with the weeds or leave one lying in the grass.

• • •

If you're like many of us, your hoses lie on the garage floor, tramped and tangled, or hang on a single spike, bent and broken. Save the time and money involved in replacing the hose. Drive three spikes into a board so each spike is one point of a triangle. Cut three short sections of hose from that one you ruined by hanging it over the single spike. Cover the three spikes with sections of hose. Now **hang up that new hose** — and be proud of it.

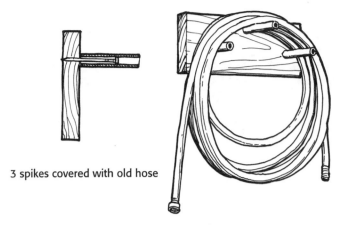

3 spikes covered with old hose

Storing the garden hose

Get a Head Start

Is it really worth the trouble to start seedlings indoors, or is it more practical to wait until spring and buy the few transplants and annuals you need? If you're willing to put in the time to reap the fun of growing your own, don't fool around with narrow windowsills and straggly plants. Grow them under lights for best results.

You can buy a plant stand for starting seedlings — or you can invest an hour in a stand that's fine for starting tomatoes and all the rest. You need:

- Four 2" x 4" x 72" uprights
- Nine 3" x 2" x 48" horizontal pieces
- Four 1" x 6" x 48" sides of plant area
- One 48" x 48" particle-board or plywood shelf
- One 60" x 60" plastic sheet, for shelf covering
- Two 48" two-tube fluorescent units with hooks and chains

Optional:
- One 2" x 2" x 96" to be cut into four supports

Use wood screws throughout. Construct shelf frame and end units, then place shelf at a height comfortable for you. Screw the two top bars into position. Mount steel hooks into the underside of the top

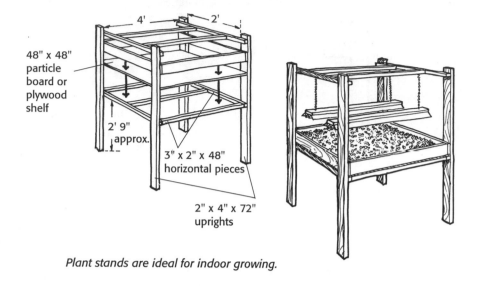

48" x 48" particle board or plywood shelf

4'

2'

2' 9" approx.

3" x 2" x 48" horizontal pieces

2" x 4" x 72" uprights

Plant stands are ideal for indoor growing.

bars so that light units suspended from them will be centered. Attach shelf to frame and add 1" **x** 6" side pieces. Place the plastic sheet inside the shelf unit and fill it with peat moss. Keep the peat moss damp to increase humidity around the plants.

Buying 48-inch-long shop lights is a lot cheaper than buying fancy plant lights from a garden shop. Replace one fluorescent tube in each fixture with a grow-light. Keep a distance of 5 to 6 inches from plant foliage to the reflector and give plants 14 to 15 hours of light each day.

• • •

The traditional way to start garden seeds indoors relied on planting the seeds in flats and transplanting them to pots. You can eliminate the transplanting step by planting seeds directly into a **plug flat.** These rigid flats have small molded pots built into the flat. Simply fill the individual plugs and sow the seeds. When the plants are large enough just pop them from the flat and plant in the garden. Plug flats come in many sizes to fit just about all types of garden crops and flowers.

• • •

Seeds often need uniform heat to germinate well. An easy way to give the seeds the warmth they need is to **put seed flats on top of the** refrigerator. The heat from the refrigerator will warm the soil and encourage rapid germination.

• • •

Leeks are one vegetable worth starting indoors. Their seedlings are so small they'd otherwise get lost among garden weeds, and you'd find yourself pulling up all the leeks — and then you'd want to pull out your hair, as well. Plant seeds anytime from January on and transplant to a trench when the garden is ready. Apply fine mulch to thwart weeds from the start.

Parsley, too, is a good indoor candidate. Plant in March and set out at the same time as leeks.

• • •

Winter squash needs to have time to ripen completely before first frost. Otherwise, the meat is light covered, not nutty and flavorful, and the squash won't keep well. In northern climates, give winter squash a head start. Start indoors six weeks before setting out. "We ate our last winter squash in early July," says a gardener who can testify to the keeping qualities of squash started in this way.

Start watermelons early, too, and when you move them to the garden, plant through holes in black plastic and give them plenty of water.

• • •

You ask for trouble if you use garden soil for indoor planting. It's likely to be loaded with pathogens. Use sterile, commercial **potting mix,** or make your own:

> two parts soil
> one part compost or leaf mold
> one part sand, perlite, or vermiculite
> one tablespoon bone meal per quart

Sterilize it in a 150°F oven for one-half hour (which may drive everyone out of the house holding their noses). To stay in your family's good graces, use a microwave oven for speedy sterilization. Put the soil in a plastic bag in which you've punched a few holes. Bake it in the microwave for four or five minutes.

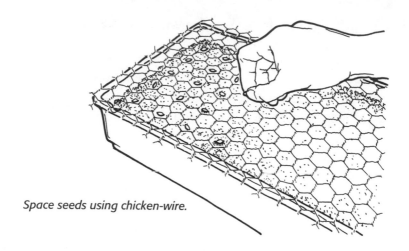

Space seeds using chicken-wire.

Systems save time. To aid in **spacing seeds in flats,** cut a piece of one-inch-mesh chicken wire the size of a flat. (Put it in a wooden frame, if you want to be fancy.) Lay it on the soil and plant a seed inside each hole for one-inch spacing. You can also plant on two-inch or three-inch centers.

•　•　•

Foil damping-off organisms, which cause young seedlings to keel over. Plant seeds in a flat, then sprinkle a one-quarter to one-half-inch layer of vermiculite over the surface. Cover with newspaper to hold in moisture until germination. Remove newspaper when seedlings show. Bottom-water to keep top layer of vermiculite dry and prevent young plants from biting the dust. Between waterings, mist lightly.

•　•　•

When it's time to **thin young seedlings** grown indoors, snip off at soil level with scissors instead of disturbing roots by pulling.

•　•　•

In January, start indoors at least two dozen seeds of **Alpine straw-berries.** By late May, you'll have small plants that can be tucked in wherever you have places to fill in the vegetable or flower garden. These beautiful perennial plants will reward you another way — pick and eat their sweet inch-long fruit throughout the summer as you garden.

A PORTABLE COLD FRAME

Phil Viereck has built a versatile, portable, insulated cold frame that enables him to eat early lettuce. He plants a crop in September and plops the cold frame over it later, to take it through the winter. "I'm convinced that what saves the lettuce is that it doesn't have extreme changes of temperature quickly," he says. "My biggest problem is remembering to open the glass on warm days. One year I cooked the whole batch." Barring that, Phil eats lettuce by April 20.

He plants his first spring crop in late March. "I've even sprinkled the seed on ice," he says. In late April, he moves the cold frame to this planting. Later, he sets it over Early Girl tomatoes.

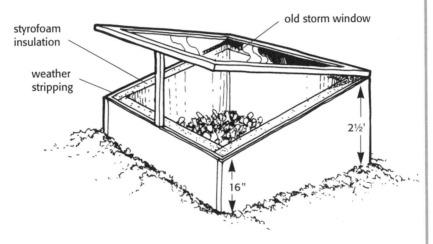

The only problem with cold frames has been the need to ventilate them to control the temperature. This opening and closing of the frame lid gets boring really fast. Instead of doing this job by hand install a **solar-powered vent control.** These gadgets were designed to use the energy of sunlight to operate controls that open and close greenhouse vents. They are just as effective in regulating cold frame temperatures.

Get **early spring lettuce** with little effort. In the fall, punch holes in two plastic containers, dish pan size if you can find them. Put six inches of a rich mixture of topsoil and compost in them, and store them in the cellar or garage. In late winter, moisten the soil well, then sow leaf lettuce to get plants two inches apart. Cover with clear plastic and keep under fluorescent lights 12 to 18 hours a day. Remove the plastic when the seedings appear. As soon as possible, move them outdoors or, better yet, into a cold frame, at least during the daylight hours. You'll be eating this lettuce in less than two months. At first, harvest to thin the plants to six inches apart, then cut off individual plants one inch above the surface of the soil, so they can grow again. Two containers should keep a small family in lettuce until the regular garden crop is ready. Experiment with varieties. Buttercrunch, Grand Rapids, and Salad Bowl grow well together.

• • •

The fastest way to heat the soil of the garden in spring is to use a **clear plastic mulch.** Clear plastic allows sunlight to pass through the plastic to heat the soil and then traps that heat near the ground. Clear plastic mulch isn't used much to heat the soil because it also stimulates rapid weed growth. Black plastic stops weed growth but does not heat the soil as effectively as clear plastic. Now the best of both products have been combined in a mulch called IRT-76 wavelength selective mulch. This product allows the strongest warming rays of the sun to pass through it and warm the soil while blocking the light that weed seeds use to germinate.

• • •

"I've eliminated the time-consuming fuss of moving **tomato seedlings** from flats to small pots to larger pots before setting them in the garden," says Closey Dickey. Plant tomato seeds directly in soil mix in-half-gallon milk cartons. Thin to one seedling per carton. When setting out plants, simply slice off the bottom of the carton and slide it up to make a protective collar.

• • •

Give hard-coated seeds a jump on germination. Nick them with a file, then before planting soak for forty-eight hours in a solution of one teaspoon Adolph's Meat Tenderizer to one quart water.

To Stake or Not to Stake

Under most circumstances, staking newly transplanted trees is a waste of time. The wind moving the trunk of unstaked trees encourages a thicker stem and sturdier growth than that achieved in staked trees. Stake only in windy locations.

How you handle vining crops, such as peas, pole beans, tomatoes, cucumbers, squash, and melons depends on your attitude toward the garden as well as the space you have available. As you plan the layout of next year's plot, choose a system that suits your gardening style.

Advantages
- Fruit is cleaner and less susceptible to damage from rotting, insects, or slugs.
- More air and sunlight reach the plants, reducing likelihood of fungus or mildew infection.
- Cultivating and harvesting are easier.
- Less space is used.
- Yields are generally higher (unless you prune).

Disadvantages
- More frequent watering is required. (Mulch to offset this.)
- More time is involved in preparing props for vertical growing. (But it may save time later.)
- Trained plants that are pruned (tomatoes) have reduced yields.
- Pruned tomatoes have more incidence of sunscald, cracking, and blossom-end rot.

• • •

Some gardeners can't be bothered with vertical growing. "We **don't stake tomatoes,** either the determinate [bushy] or the indeterminate [viney] varieties. Nor do we bother to mulch under them," says Tom Foster, a gardener with a relaxed attitude and plenty of space. "We overplant. We have so many, so if we lose some, what difference does it make?"

"I don't have the time, and don't want to take the time, to stake," says a golfer-gardener. "I let the tomatoes sprawl. In mid-July, when the soil is thoroughly warm, I put black plastic under them."

Others feel that tiptoeing through tomato or cucumber vines, bending and stooping, searching for ripe ones, stepping on some in the process, and coping with slug holes, rabbit nibbles, and rot is not their idea of lazy gardening. They'd rather spend a little time in winter preparing supports and later enjoy their investment with a more organized garden. Supports should be ready to go into the garden at the same time as seeds or plants.

· · ·

You don't know the **difference between determinate and indeterminate** plants?

Most early tomatoes are of the **determinate** type, with short stems and fewer than three leaves on the vine between flower clusters. Determinate tomato plants grow naturally bushy and don't need pruning. They tend to make their growth and then have all the fruit that is set ripen.

Late varieties are usually **indeterminate.** Their stems grow indefinitely, and the fruit ripens over a longer period. Indeterminate varieties respond well to pruning and vertical training.

Keep Tomatoes Upright

Have all the advantages of vertical growing without the bother of pruning and tying: grow your tomatoes in **cages.** Buy them commercially or construct sturdier ones yourself. Use concrete-reinforcing wire with six-inch mesh. (Wire used for cages should have openings large enough for your hand to reach through for harvesting.) For each cage, cut a section of wire five feet three inches long: the three-inch pieces can be hooked to the other end of the mesh to form the cylinder. Each cylinder holds one plant. You can make the diameter of the cylinder larger (three to four feet) and put three plants inside. Open the cylinders and store flat in winter.

This wire cylinder and the wooden cage on the opposite page give all the benefits of vertical growing, without the bother of pruning and tying.

Avoid the possibility of a tumbled cage by driving one **stake into the ground** next to the cage and attaching with wire.

• • •

A wooden cage is a variation on wire.

• • •

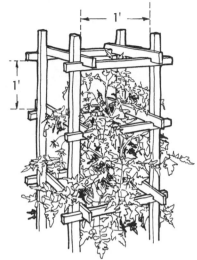

Support tomatoes between two **parallel fences** eighteen to twenty-four inches apart. To make the fences, nail or staple five-foot high hog wire with four-inch mesh to sturdy stakes. Drive stakes into the ground. Plant tomatoes between the fences. As they grow, slide cross-sticks between the fences for additional support.

Wooden cage

Parallel fences provide much-needed support for tomatoes.

Wooden tents are a simple method to keep tomatoes upright. These are constructed of 1" x 2" lumber and fold flat for winter storage.

Train indeterminate (vining) varieties on string. Set six-foot high fence posts six feet apart. Stretch sturdy wire between the tops of the posts. Plant tomatoes eighteen inches apart under the wire. Over each plant, tie one end of a piece of twine to the wire and the other end to the bottom of the plant As the tomato grows, prune it to a single stem and train it to the twine. "You soon learn to twist the string around the tomato, not the tomato around the string, or the tomato breaks," cautions County Agent John Page, who uses this system in his own garden.

Training on twine works well for vining varieties.

Still bent on conventional staking? Bob Kolkebeck buys 1" x 2" lumber in twelve-foot lengths. He cuts it in two at an angle, creating a ready-made point that drives easily into the ground and saves a few minutes of his time.

Conventional stakes drive easily into the ground if cut at an angle.

• • •

Take a minute to make a figure-eight when you tie a tomato stem to a stake. Loop the tie loosely around the stem, cross it, and tie securely to the sake. Then the tie doesn't become a tourniquet for the plant.

A figure-eight tomato tie lets the plant grow unencumbered.

• • •

By the time my sheets are ready for the rag bag, they are so weak they break every time I try to use them for plant ties. I've had better luck with pre-cut **plastic-covered twistems,** 13½ inches long. They are reusable. Collect and straighten at the end of the season. Or use soft and stretchy strips cut from discarded nylon stockings.

Ingenious Pea Supports

Too lazy to put in pea fences? **Prop up vines with piles of hay,** à la Ruth Stout.

• • •

Plant **dwarf peas,** those that grow only fifteen to eighteen inches high, in rows five to six inches apart or in a six-inch wide trench. Plants will intertwine and hold each other up.

Prepare pea fencing ahead of time and save work in the spring. Here's how Bob and Eleanor Kolkebeck assemble their fence for edible-podded peas, which need a **tall and sturdy support.**

Staple six-foot high, two-inch-mesh chicken wire to six-foot lengths of 1" x 2" lumber. Put the lumber at each end of the fence and space it at three- to four-foot intervals in between. Roll it up and store it until planting time.

In spring, unroll the fence and lay it on the ground with one edge touching the planting trench. Wherever there is a lumber strip, drive a three- to four-foot high metal fence post into the ground (much easier to drive than wood).

Raise the chicken wire fence against the metal stakes. Wire the metal stakes to the wooden fence posts, using about three twistems for each stake. You need a friend to help juggle everything. At the end of the pea season, untwist the wires, pull up the stakes, roll the chicken wire and lumber neatly, and store until next year.

"One year we had a heavy windstorm, and it blew all the pea vines off the fence. We had a lovely fence standing, but all the vines were in a tangled heap on the ground, impossible to put up again. Now we take a few minutes to prevent this. As the vines grow, we simply hold them with twine every foot or two of growth as insurance," Eleanor explains. Fasten one end to the first stake, stretch it to the next and wind it around, and so on. Do this on both sides of the fence.

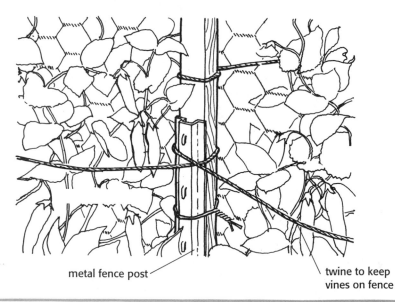

metal fence post

twine to keep vines on fence

Use **pea brush** as our forefathers did. Just after planting, stick twigs of deciduous trees or shrubs into the pea trench. Place them close together so they form a natural latticework for pea vines to climb. After the peas are harvested, just toss the branches in the chipper or brush pile.

. . .

For **conventional pea fencing,** stretch chicken wire on metal fence posts. Make it three to four feet high for regular peas and six or more feet high for the edible-podded variety.

BEAN POLES

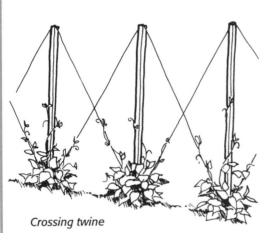

Set eight-foot high wooden poles three feet apart. Run twine from the top of each pole to the bottom of the adjacent poles, forming Xs for extra climbing space for the beans.

Crossing twine

Save your Christmas trees for bean poles. In our garden, we drive six-foot high metal fence posts into the ground and, with twistems, attach a Christmas tree, its branches cut to short stubs, to extend two feet above the tops of the metal posts. The roughness of the stubby tree trunk provides a good grip for the bean vines, and the metal post the sturdiness they require. (Collect unsold Christmas trees from local markets immediately after Christmas to prepare summer bean poles and use the sheared-off branches as winter protection for perennials.)

Old Christmas tree

Bean Poles

Poles for pole beans must be anchored well — two feet into the ground — or they'll blow over in a summer thunderstorm. Instead of going to all that work, tie three poles together at the top, spread them **tepee** fashion, then push the bottoms into the soil and plant around them. Children love the natural tepee they form.

CUCUMBER TRELLISES

Ray Lambert uses an old metal **clothesline support.** He drives two stakes under the outer edges of the T and runs twine, just above the ground, from them to the center post. He pokes pieces of twine through the holes in the cross piece of the support and attaches them to the ground string. Under each vertical length of twine he plants a cucumber seed.

Old clothes line pole

A-frame

Make an **A-frame** for cucumber or squash vines. Construct two wooden rectangles, attach hog wire or nylon trellis netting to the frames, and hinge at the top.

Train Those Cucumbers!

Use a concrete-reinforcing **wire cage** (as described for tomatoes) three or four feet in diameter. Plant cucumber seeds around the circumference. (Use the inside as a collector for composting materials and toss in a bit of manure, to feed the cukes.)

Props for Floppy Flowers

Make **cylinders** of varying heights from green plastic-coated pea fencing with 2" x 2½" mesh. Place over plants in early spring, before they are more than a few inches high. As the perennials grow, their foliage pokes through the mesh so the cylinder is hardly noticeable. (If you wait until the plant needs staking, you may break it as you try to wiggle the cylinder over it, and it will never look natural.) For most plants, there's no need to attach the cylinder to the ground. Occasionally, a heavy delphinium may tip it over. Just poke a stake through the mesh and into the ground. this system works for any "clumpy" plant, such a coreopsis, gallardia, baby's breath, or delphinium.

Wire cylinder

• • •

Straighten the hook of a wire coat hanger and pull the long side of the triangle up to form a diamond. Stick the straightened hook wire into the ground and use two or three to prop up floppy plants. Prepare a supply now to have handy when you need them.

• • •

For peonies, cut circles of chicken wire the diameter of each peony clump. Drive one stake behind the clump and very early, when sprouts are emerging from the ground, lay the circle over them and the stake. As the peonies grow, let the chicken wire circle rise to keep them from sprawling.

Peony prop

There are many ways to extend the growing season from cold frames to row covers. But the easiest way to add two weeks to the growing season is to **do nothing at all.** Nature has taken care of it for you. In the last fifteen years the growing season in most of the northern hemisphere has arrived about ten days earlier in the spring and lasted about four days longer in the fall. Scientists aren't sure why this is so, but it is.

Dig In!

BIRDSONG FILLS the air, and the yearning to plant consumes you. Here's where restraint is needed, before the elixir of damp earth intoxicates you. Chant "Wait, wait," and check to see if the soil is dry enough to be worked. Scoop up a handful and squeeze. Open your hand. If the soil sticks together, it is still too wet. If it crumbles, it is ready.

Never work wet soil, especially clay. You may ruin its structure for the entire season and end up tripping over solid, sun-baked clods instead of early lettuce.

Did you incorporate lots of organic matter into the soil in fall? If you do that every year, you will find increasing ease of preparation in spring, as your soil becomes more spongy and fluffy. It will also be ready to work earlier in the spring.

Varieties: What to Plant

Plant **pole beans** instead of bush beans. Pole beans yield up to twice as many beans as bush varieties and have better flavor to boot.

• • •

For the **fastest crop of carrots,** plant small-rooted varieties that are ready to pull in half the time.

• • •

To avoid thinning carrots, plant **pelleted seed.** Space seed 2 inches apart in rows.

• • •

To grow **straight, well-shaped eggplant,** train slender-fruited varieties to a trellis. As the fruit matures it hangs down from the vine, growing into a slender, straight shape.

Timing: When to Plant

Cool weather crops — peas, spinach, lettuce, onions, garlic, and brassicas — can go in as soon as the ground can be worked. The gardening books say beets, carrots, chard, and radishes can be sown in cold soil, but every time I have tried that, they have been decimated by tiny, flea-like insects. They seem to appreciate a couple of week's grace.

If you're a lazy gardener, you won't try to plant the rest of your garden too early. If the seeds manage to sprout before rotting in cold soil, the plants will probably struggle, and you will fuss and sputter. Most crops need soil that has warmed up.

Find out the average date of the last spring frost in your area (ask your Agricultural Extension Agent). Wait until then to plant beans, sweet corn, and New Zealand spinach.

Crops that need thoroughly warm soil are cucumbers, squash, melons, tomatoes, peppers, eggplants, and lima beans. Wait at least a week after the average date of the last frost before setting them in the garden (unless you are willing to provide hotcaps or some other kind of protection).

• • •

To **warm up soil** more quickly for heat-loving crops, spread clear plastic over the ground until planting time. (It lets in more heat than black plastic.)

• • •

For an **extended pea season,** plant early, midseason, and late varieties at the same time, as soon as the soil can be worked. This gives better results than successive plantings of one variety. Peas of one variety tend to catch up with brethren planted earlier. Two weeks difference in planting may mean only one day's difference in harvesting. This principle applies to corn, as well.

• • •

Plant corn when apple blossoms begin to fall.

• • •

In the North, **turnips** planted in spring don't do well. If you have trouble, plant in mid-July for a fall crop.

• • •

Cole crops (cabbage, broccoli, cauliflower, Brussels sprouts, collards) do best in fall. "They love cold weather," says John Page,

Bennington (Vermont) County Extension Agent. He plants these seeds in his garden in mid-July and transplants them to available spaces any time from mid-August to Labor Day.

WIDE ROWS

After preparing the seedbed, run string attached to two stakes across the garden. Line up one edge of a steel garden rake next to the string and drag it the length of the row. For a wider row, lay out two strings to the desired width and drag the rake between them.

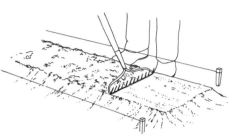

Smoothing ground

Broadcast seed in the raked area, slightly closer together than you would in a conventional row. Press into soil with the back of a hoe or rake.

With the rake or hoe, pull soil from outside the row to cover the seed. (Use enough soil to make a covering four times the seed's diameter, or for long seeds, as deep as their length. In clay soil, you can cover a little more sparingly than in sandy soil.) Tamp again. You can cover a planting of fine seeds with a thin layer of straw to help hold in moisture until germination.

Scattering seeds

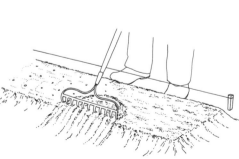

Tamping in

Raking soil to cover

Raised Beds

Using the conventional method, soil preparation for raised beds was a lot of work. It involved double-digging, the contemplation of which would send any lazy gardener to the nearest hammock, plus spading in compost, well-rotted manure, bone meal, wood ashes, and more manure.

There's an easier way. Start with a well-prepared seedbed, but it needn't be double-dug. Enrich it with compost, manure, other organic matter or fertilizer. The raised beds can be formed with either hand tools or a tiller with hilling attachment.

Using hand tools

1. Mark the bed with stakes and strings. Dick Raymond, author of *Joy of Gardening,* suggests sixteen inches as a good width. Some gardeners prefer beds three or four feet wide. Make them any convenient length. Walkways can be up to twenty inches wide. (One gardener makes them the width of a bale of hay for efficient mulching of walks.)

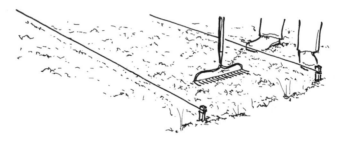

2. Use a rake to pull soil from the walkway to the top of the bed. Stand in one walkway and draw soil toward you from the opposite walkway. After completing one side, do the same from the other side.

3. Level the top of the bed with the back of the rake. Sides should slope at a forty-five-degree angle. A lip of soil around the top edge of a new bed will help reduce erosion.

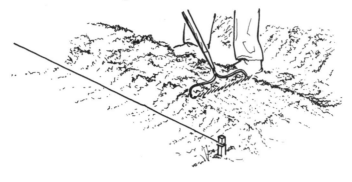

Using a tiller

1. Stake out walkways of two tiller widths.

2. Attach furrowing and hilling attachment to the tiller. Set hilling wings to the highest position, so they will push soil upward onto the bed.

3. Hill-up beds. Line up the center of the tiller in front of the first stake, point it at the stake at the other end of the bed, and guide tiller directly toward it. Repeat on the other side.

4. Smooth the top of the bed with a rake.

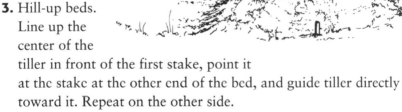

Raised bed in cross section

To plant raised beds, broadcast small seeds as you would for a wide row. Larger seeds such as for bush beans or transplants such as cabbage should be spaced the distances recommended for a conventional row, but the spacing should be in a pattern that lets the leaves of mature plants barely touch one another, providing a living mulch.

Square Beds

The first year, till the entire garden space and mix organic matter into it before you lay out the four-foot by four-foot beds with walkways in between. In subsequent years, use hand tools to prepare and plant one four-by-four block at a time. First, divide it in quarters with string or by drawing in the soil. Then divide each of the four squares you have created into four more squares. Now you have sixteen planting units, each one foot square. Plant the recommended number of seeds or transplants within that one-foot square:

- 16 carrots, beets, onions, or radishes
- 9 bush beans or spinach
- 4 lettuce, parsley, or Swiss chard
- 1 broccoli, cabbage, cauliflower, corn, eggplant, or pepper

Summer squash and zucchini, of course, would never make it in a one-foot square. Give them more space. Grow tomatoes and vining crops like cucumbers, winter squash, pole beans, and peas on vertical supports.

Whenever you harvest from a one-foot square, add organic matter, such as compost or well-rotted manure, or fertilizer and dig it in with a trowel. That keeps the soil ready for planting, and preparation is never a major project.

Let Others Do the Work

Have you selected a **new garden site,** and now you want to prepare it? You can spade it, but that's hard work. Try covering it with black plastic. In one month, and often less, all plant life under the plastic will die, and the soil will have a delightfully soft moist quality. For a much more thorough job, put a hog or two in the area. Pigs will prepare the area more completely than a rototiller. They will eat all the weeds and their roots and will turn over the soil — and fertilize it.

Row Markers — Look, Ma, No Strings!

A picket fence on a hoe? I glanced at the weird contraption lying on the ground next to Ray Lambert's garden. "That's my row marker," he chuckled. "My grandfather had a homemade row marker. I used features of his and added my own ideas."

To the blade of an old garden hoe he attached horizontally a three-foot length of 1" x 2" lumber. On either end, he centered a one-foot length of lumber, pointed on each end like a picket fence, perpendicular to the first piece. Protruding from the underside, at one foot intervals, are two more pointed pieces, each six inches long.

Ray combines elements of wide row, raised-bed, and square-bed methods in his garden. He can use the side of the row marker with three-foot spacing to lay out a three-foot-wide row, or to mark the location of two rows of strawberry plants three feet apart.

He can flip the marker over and pull it carefully down the center of a raised bed to mark out-one-foot spacing, then pull it across the bed at right angles to the first set of marks to make a grid. If he needs six-inch spacing, he can move the marker over for a second pull halfway between the first marks.

His versatile and efficient tool eliminates tedious measuring and stretching of strings.

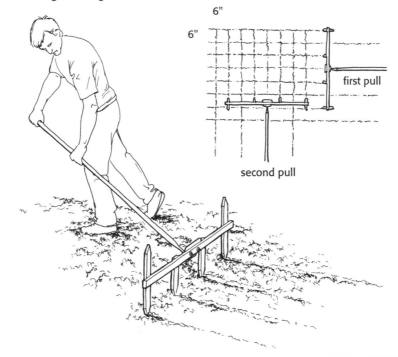

6"

6"

first pull

second pull

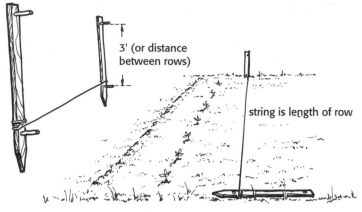

3' (or distance between rows)

string is length of row

Marking stake with twine

"I made this set of garden stakes that also can be used for measuring," explains one gardener. If you're too lazy to put the pegs in the stakes at the proper distances for your garden, just mark on the stakes with an indelible pencil. Once built, your stakes and your twine are always right there, ready for use.

• • •

Use a little **lime** to mark each row before making the furrow — especially good for lime-lovers like lettuce, beets, and spinach.

• • •

Drop a few **radish seeds** in each row as you plant. They will germinate quickly to remind you that something else is planted there. Because they mature so quickly, they serve as a thinning device, since they leave space for the main crop as they are harvested.

Dealing with Tiny Seeds

How to avoid thinning or how to thin easily **small-seeded vegetables** like carrots, lettuce, and parsley is a problem all gardeners face. There is more than one solution:

- Broadcast plantings can be thinned with a rake. Draw a metal garden rake across the wide row or raised bed when seedlings are little — under one inch tall. Let the rake tines penetrate the soil one-quarter to one-half inch.

- "Planting seeds thinly and carefully takes a lot less time than laborious thinning after the plants come up," insists one **precise gardener.** He's a natural for square-bed planting, in which each seed is planted singly and spaced carefully.
- Figure out how much seed you need to plant one row or bed and mix that amount with sand or dirt. Sow evenly.

"Don't plant too thickly, period," John Page argues. "I can take a package of carrot seeds and make them go from here to Chicago. Most people want a little row of carrots. They have a big package of carrot seed. They think they have to plant all of the seeds in that little row. It's no more trouble to plant them an inch apart. If you must thin, do it when they're little. If you wait 'til they're too big, you're a dead duck. When the seedlings are one inch tall, it won't look as though there are any carrots left after you've thinned."

• • •

"We plant sparingly to start with and don't thin until the tiny carrots [or lettuce or spinach] are big enough to eat," says one efficient gardener. **"Thin and eat** — no wasted energy."

• • •

Buy "pre-spaced" **seed tapes** or pelleted seeds (small seeds with a coating that increases their size and makes them easier to plant sparingly). These both cost more than regular seed.

• • •

Unless you have knee-deep, soft soil, don't try to grow commercial varieties of **carrots,** or they will fork and split and come out of the soil looking like freaks. Choose a variety to suit the soil — half-longs are best for most home gardens, and Royal Chantenays for heavy, clay soil.

• • •

Even in a **conventional garden layout,** never plant little things like beets, carrots, or onions in widely spaced rows. Instead, plant three or four rows six inches apart, then leave an alleyway. One practical gardener plants three rows of beets six inches apart, pulls the middle row for greens, and lets the two outer rows mature for roots.

• • •

Try a wide-row or raised-bed **salad garden.** In a bucket, mix seeds of spinach, chard, assorted leaf lettuces, beets, and radishes. Broadcast and later thin with a rake. The radishes are ready first. When you pull them, you make space. Next comes young spinach. Pull some of that to make space. From then on, just cut off the tops of everything for a continuous crop of greens. Plant a good-sized salad bed in the spring and two smaller ones during the summer. When the chard gets too big to eat raw, cook it.

• • •

Cover little seeds with compost when planting. Compost holds moisture, is less likely to form a crust, and provides a nutritional boost.

• • •

Seeds won't germinate in dry ground. **Keep seedbed moist** after planting.

24 Planting Hints

1. **Soak seeds** of beets, Swiss chard, and peas for fifteen or twenty minutes before planting. Soak parsley, New Zealand spinach, and celery seed overnight to hasten germination.

2. Make **multiple plantings** of lettuce. "I make nine plantings of lettuce each season," says a Vermont gardener. "Sometimes I scrape snow away to plant the first batch." He plants only a couple of feet of each variety at a time. "I don't try to salvage overmature lettuce," he declares. "I turn it under and plant some more."

3. **Looseleaf lettuces** are quicker and easier to grow than heading types. Plant Romaine for a crunchy, meatier leaf that does quite well in hot weather.

4. Start seed of **buttercrunch** lettuce in beds. Transplant seedlings eight inches apart to all the empty spaces in the garden — next to the peas, between rows of onions, or between young brassicas.

5. Plant **early lettuce** between asparagus rows.

6. Having **trouble starting lettuce** in hot weather? Since it germinates best in cool ground, Ruth Stout chills the seed in the refrigerator, plants it, then lays blocks of ice over it, and insulates from the sun with feed bags. Try this with late plantings of spinach or peas, too.

7. **Does spinach bolt** too soon in your garden? Try New Zealand spinach or grow Malabar spinach on a fence or trellis.

8. Leaf crops — lettuce, spinach, chard, mustard greens, and parsley — do well in partially **shaded locations.**

9. Always inoculate your legume seed before planting. You can buy **legume inoculant,** which looks like black powder, through seed catalogs or from feed stores. It adds a fresh culture of nitrogen-fixing bacteria to the seed, which will increase yield and quality of peas and beans. Moisten seeds and shake with the powder just before planting. A touch of honey on the seeds makes the powder stick better. Keep unused inoculant in the refrigerator until you need it again. There is also a granular type that is sprinkled in furrows as you sow.

10. For **earliest peas,** prepare the planting trench in fall. In spring, just push seed into the soil.

11. Mark Hebert isn't a lazy gardener. He loves it out there in his large and beautiful garden. But let's say that Mark doesn't believe in doing things the hard way. And when it comes to **raising peas** Mark has an easy way: "Early in the season, till up a ten-foot square of your garden. Scatter on it one pound of a shorter-bushed pea, such as Little Marvel. Till or rake in the peas, then walk over the soil. And that's it until two months later then you return to harvest them — and you should harvest fifty pounds of pods from that tiny space. No need for fences or other supports — the peas will support each other." Try this just once, and you'll never go back to the single-row system, trying to get each pea just three inches apart from its neighbor.

12. For the vegetable that requires the least effort to grow, we'll nominate the **Jerusalem artichoke.** Plant a few tubers in a bed in one corner of your garden. And that's it. They need little or no care — the greatest effort probably goes into keeping them from taking over your entire garden. They'll easily discourage the advances of the hungriest insects. Dig them up in the fall or early spring. You'll miss a few — and they'll grow to provide your crop for the next season. They're delicious and nutritious, fresh or cooked.

13. **Lima beans need warm soil.** Pre-sprout seeds before planting to reduce chances of their rotting in the garden. Start them in deep flats in vermiculite or perlite. Limas are "iffy" in the North. One year we had a super crop of sweet, tender beans. The next two years, August was wet and cold and the pods never filled, so we reluctantly decided not to give them garden space.

14. For the direct seeding of **brassicas** without laborious thinning, put sticks in the ground eighteen inches apart. Plant a few seeds by each stick. Gradually thin to one plant by snipping off seedlings at ground level. Plant the empty spots between the sticks with lettuce or spinach, which will be harvested by the time the brassicas need more space.

15. Plant **collards.** You don't have to fight the cabbage worm.

16. Learn to recognize "volunteers." Once you plant **dill,** you'll never have to plant it again. Let seeds from a few flower heads scatter each year. Be alert for the feathery green tufts that emerge the following spring and save a few when you cultivate or mulch.

17. Have **potatoes without digging.** Place seed potatoes one foot apart on top of last year's mulch, or on a fall deposit of a few inches of leaves, preferably shredded. Cover with a foot of loose hay. When the tops die down, just rake off the hay.

You can even steal a few new potatoes during the season without hurting the plant. Carefully lift the hay when potato blossoms begin to drop, break off tiny potatoes from the mother plant and replace the hay.

18. Make sure **onion** necks are exposed to sun and not covered with dirt. By harvest time, they will already be partly dried.

19. For **cucumber flavor** without cucumber vines, plant the annual herb borage or the perennial salad burnet. Mince and add to salads.

BLOCKS OF CORN

"Corn takes a lot out of the soil. It can take a lot out of the gardener, too, if you don't do it right," says a knowledgeable one. To satisfy corn's voracious appetite, dig manure into the soil in spring and give booster feedings when it is eight to ten inches high and again when silk forms.

Corn is wind-pollinated. The male flower is the tassel, the female flower the silk. Every kernel has a silk attached to it. Undeveloped kernels on a cob mean they weren't fertilized. To ensure complete pollination, don't plant corn in one long row. Planting in blocks is best. Here's how one gardener plants corn in raised beds:

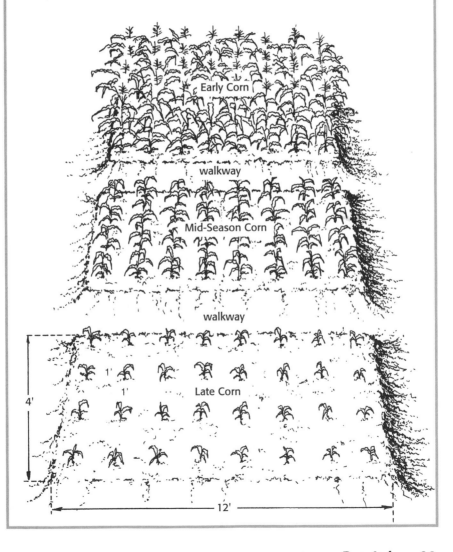

20. Stick seeds of **winter squash** in a partly finished compost pile. The squash plants camouflage the pile, which gives the squashes nourishment and the room they need to sprawl. I have vowed never again to let squash grow freely in my garden after the vines from one hill took over a fifteen-by-fifteen-foot space, smothering everything in their path!

21. If you do let **winter squash** trail, leave a minimum of five feet between plants. "We have found fewer plants well spaced give more squash, and they are much easier to pick more quickly," says a gardener with lots of space.

22. Interplant the second crop of **bush beans** between bands of beets and carrots. In a month, all soil is shaded and there's no place for weeds to grow.

23. Plant **cucumbers** between corn plants to give them some light shade, which they like. Both crops like heat and moisture.

24. Aim for a **three-year rotation** in your garden, in terms of the plants' needs for nutrients.

> Year One, **Heavy feeders:** corn, squash, brassicas, tomatoes, melons
>
> Year Two, **Heavy givers:** legumes (which return nitrogen to soil), such as peas, beans, alfalfa, clover, vetch
>
> Year Three, **Light feeders:** root crops, such as beets, onions, carrots, turnips, kohlrabi, parsnips
>
> Or, interplant the three types of crops in the same bed.

Take Advantage of Companion Planting

Some crops encourage or discourage each others' growth. **Good combinations** are beans and savory, tomatoes with basil or parsley, broccoli and onions, peas and carrots. **Don't** plant onions with beans or peas; they have an adverse effect on each other. (For more about companion planting, see the table on pages 108–109).

The Care and Feeding of Transplants

Always **harden off** transplants for eight to ten days before you set them out in the garden. Expose them to short then gradually longer periods outdoors. (If you purchase transplants, find out if they've been hardened off. If not, make sure you do it.)

• • •

If seedlings are in flats, **slice the roots** into squares with a knife about a week before transplanting. Repeat the process before removing from flat.

• • •

Feed transplants with **fish emulsion** the day before setting them out. If possible, **transplant on a cloudy or drizzly day.** Or set out seedlings in the late afternoon or early evening. It's more comfortable for you, and the plants will thrive without requiring shade or constant watering.

• • •

If seedlings are in **peat pots,** be sure to bury the whole pot. Otherwise peat will draw moisture from the soil to the air.

• • •

When setting out pot-bound or **root-bound transplants,** gently spread out the roots in all directions. That helps them become re-established more quickly.

• • •

Give each transplant a boost by adding a shovelful of compost or well-rotted manure mixed with some bonemeal and wood ashes to the bottom of each planting hole. Do this under tomatoes, brassicas, eggplant, cucumbers, squash, and melons.

• • •

When you try to **water transplants** with a watering can, does most of the water run off in another direction? Give each transplant its own drip-watering system. Poke a tiny hole in the bottom of a gallon-sized plastic jug. Fill with water and put next to the newly set tomato plant or in a hill of melons after the seedlings are up.

Why risk the possibility of having to replant? **Protect young plants** from being nipped by frost or nibbled by animals. Cut the bottom out of gallon-sized plastic milk jugs. Leave the cap off, for ventilation. Place over seedlings. This acts like a mini-greenhouse. You can also do this over seeds of tender crops. One gardener keeps a jug on her zucchini until the leaves push the jug off the ground.

Keep a drum of **manure tea** brewing for supplemental feeding of transplants or any green thing that needs a quick infusion. Fill a big garbage can about one-eighth full of fresh horse or cow manure, then fill the can with water. Stir occasionally and wait a week or two. This is powerful stuff. Dilute it until it's the color of weak tea before using. Add water to the can after every use. When the water is the color of weak tea, start again, after adding the spent manure to your compost pile.

Make **vegetarian tea** the same way, using stinging nettles or comfrey leaves. The latter are rich in potash, so are good for all vegetables.

A lazy gardening friend brews manure tea from his children's pet rabbit droppings in a five-gallon plastic drum with a cover.

• • •

Use a fifty-five gallon metal drum and attach a spigot and valve a few inches from the bottom of the drum. Drill a hole near the top and use an **S**-hook to suspend a container of manure inside. Fill the barrel with water.

Several gardeners who use this system tried a laundry bag for the manure at first, but the cloth disintegrated. Now they're using a

The manure tea in this 55-gallon metal drum can be delivered by hose to any crop that needs a quick boost.

different approach. They cut four rectangular holes out of a plastic bucket and put aluminum screening inside. The bucket is filled with manure and suspended in the water from the rim of the barrel.

The barrel is set on a three-foot wooden stand located at the top of the garden. A length of hose is laid out specifically for manure tea delivery. A nozzle can be attached to spray or removed to dribble manure water on transplants or any crop that needs a quick boost.

Tip-Top Tomatoes

To reduce moisture loss and encourage a strong root system, prune off all but the top rosette and the large leaves just below it. Bury the rest of the stem. If it is leggy, lay it in a trench. The tomato will put out roots all along the stem. One gardener digs a hole or trench deeper than needed, stuffs shredded newspaper in it to help hold moisture, then covers it with soil and places the transplants as usual.

• • •

Plant borage among the tomatoes **to attract bees** for early fruit set.

Ray Lambert digs out an eight- to twelve-inch deep circle four feet in diameter, fills it with manure and compost, and puts a little soil on top. He plants six early (determinate) tomato plants around the circumference of the circle and slips wire cages over them. In the center of the circle, he sets a two-foot high, two-foot diameter cylinder of pea wire. He fills it with manure and compost.

In dry weather, he lets a hose trickle into the top of the feeding cylinder. He does virtually nothing else — doesn't prune, doesn't weed, doesn't feed. The cages contain the plants, the plants are close enough together so they shade the soil and no weeds grow, and the center cylinder does the feeding.

He does the same thing with **late varieties** of tomatoes, but because they need more room, he sets only four plants around one feeding cylinder, two to three feet apart. In mid-August, he chops off the tops, so all growth goes to ripening tomatoes.

feeding cylinder

tomato cages

If you're a fisherman and sometimes get **trash fish** such as suckers, don't throw them back. Pop them into your freezer. Come planting time, think of the Indians at the Plymouth Colony, and drop them into the soil. Try placing one in a hole dug for a tomato plant, for example. Put the fish in first, then three or four inches of soil, then the plant. As an experiment, put a fish under every other tomato plant, so that you can measure the results.

Grow tomatoes in **hanging baskets** placed near the kitchen. They are good looking, easy to care for, and are easy to reach come salad time. The best varieties to grow are the sweet cherry types that will yield many delicious fruits over a long season.

Pampering Peppers

If you'll be watering your long-season crops such as tomatoes and peppers, mound up a circular dam around each plant, using your hand and a trowel. You'll spend much less time watering, and you won't be wasting the water that would spread out away from the plants.

Form a watering bowl to conserve water.

Peppers **prefer slightly acid soil.** Bury a few book matches under each pepper plant when you set them in the garden. The sulfur in the match heads will increase soil acidity. Make sure to put a bit of soil between the matches and plant's roots.

• • •

Peppers are **finicky.** They don't like cold or heat, but prefer a temperature between 53° and 85°F. Mulching plants helps maintain even temperature and moisture. Do plant in rich, well-drained soil and give lots of water.

Grow Edible Perennials

For your perennial vegetables and fruits, pick a spot separate from or on the edge of (second best) the main vegetable garden. The easiest way to get a bed started is to stake it out the season before you plant. Cover existing sod with a thick layer of newspapers, magazines, or cardboard. A friend of mine declares that covering sod is the best use she's found for cast-off issues of the Congressional Record. "They're so thick nothing will grow through them," she says. So they don't blow away, pile something on top — hay, wood chips, sawdust, branches, whatever. By spring, the sod will have decomposed and added green manure to the soil without a struggle.

Raspberries

Raspberries can be planted right through the mulch and newspapers. Simply dig out a spot for each plant and throw some compost or well-rotted manure in the bottom of the hole before setting the plant. Space plants about three feet apart. Sink red raspberries an inch or two deeper than they were in the nursery. Black or purple raspberries can be set at the same depth at which they grew.

• • •

Always **buy new plants** when you start a raspberry bed. Old ones are too likely to carry disease.

• • •

"**Be ruthless** with raspberries!" warns one lazy gardener. Plant them in one long row. Whenever suckers try to widen the boundaries of the bed, pull them out! *Never* plant more than one row wide, or soon they will grow together and you won't be able to get in to pick.

• • •

Keep a raspberry bed **heavily mulched,** six inches to a foot deep.

• • •

Raspberry canes are biennials. This year's new canes will bear next year (although everbearing varieties will produce a crop on the tips of new canes in the fall). This year's bearing canes will die after fruiting. Cut them at ground level and prune out all the weak new canes as well. In spring you can top the year-old canes so they won't flop over. Remember — **be ruthless!**

Prop canes by driving posts at six-foot intervals on either side of the bed and stringing two courses of wire between them, one at about knee level, the other chest-high.

• • •

Don't waste time on any but the two best varieties of purple raspberries: Royalty and Brandywine.

Place posts at six-foot intervals to support raspberry canes.

Strawberries Simplified

Growing strawberries always sounds complicated. To grow them successfully, you need a good system. This year's producing plant will send out runners during the summer. For best fruit, limit the "babies" you allow to grow probably to two or four per plant. At the end of each season pull up the mother plants.

Set out new plants four feet apart when leaves of trees begin to unfurl in spring. The first summer, remove all blossoms so that the strength of the plant goes to sending out vigorous runners.

Keep strawberries heavily mulched, preferably with a weed-free material such as straw, salt hay, wood chips, sawdust, or pine needles.

Here's how Closey Dickey put in a new raised strawberry bed. In late summer, she laid out a bed seventy-five feet long and four or five feet wide and covered it thickly with newspaper. On either edge, on top of the newspaper, she laid bales of hay, end to end. In the two-foot space between the bales, she piled manure, peat moss, topsoil, bone meal and greensand. From time to time until winter, she stirred this brew.

In fall's crisp weather, her husband set 2" x 6" pressure-treated landscape boards in the ground, against the hay, for a frame to keep grass out and mulch in.

In early spring, the Dickeys planted two rows of strawberry plants down the middle of the bed and snipped all blooms that first summer. On either side runners went into the hay, which by now had disintegrated.

Each spring, Closey will take out two-year-old plants and let new runners become established. One year she will have two rows producing in the center, the next year one row on either edge.

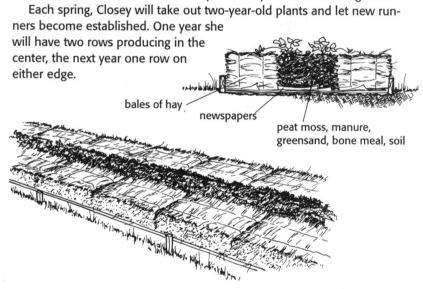

bales of hay

newspapers

peat moss, manure, greensand, bone meal, soil

Blueberries

Blueberries need an acid soil, a pH of 5 to 5.6. They are completely intolerant of limey soil, so if that's what yours is, the laziest way to have blueberries is to buy them at the market.

If you have soil with almost enough acidity, dig in peat, pine needles, or cottonseed meal to increase it. Blueberries like soil high in organic matter. They have few insect pests. Plant them in groups to encourage pollination. (They're not self-pollinating, meaning a single blueberry plant cannot fertilize itself.) Mulch heavily with pine needles.

Asparagus

Buy one-year-old roots. Years ago, it seems, gardeners would dig a trench to China in which to set their asparagus. Lazy gardeners don't bother to dig one that deep, but asparagus are heavy feeders, so you should get some nourishment under their roots at planting time. Dig ten to twelve inches deep and about a foot wide. Lay down four or five inches of compost or well-rotted manure before setting the roots so that they are about six inches below ground level. You can make a little cone of soil under each crown and spread the roots out over it. Set them two feet apart in rows four or five feet apart. Cover with two inches of soil and, during the summer, gradually draw more soil back into the row as the plants grow.

• • •

Grow many more spears from the same amount of space by planting **all-male varieties.** These cultivars bear thicker, more numerous spears because they don't go to seed. Some all-male varieties include 'Jersey Giant' and 'Jersey Knight'.

• • •

As tempting as it may be to cut and sample young spears, restrain that impulse. The **plants need two seasons** to grow and build strength before you begin harvesting.

• • •

"The **secret to asparagus** is to fertilize it lavishly," explains a gardener whose succulent spears are known throughout her neighborhood. Feed first in early spring at the same time you cultivate, and again when you stop harvesting. After the ground freezes, load up the bed with manure.

Rhubarb

Rhubarb is attractive enough to use as part of your ornamental landscaping. It, too, is a heavy feeder. Dig a generous planting hole, fill it with compost or well-rotted manure, and set roots so that the uppermost buds are two to three inches below the soil surface. Add more rich organic matter each year. Be sure to remove flower stalks as soon as they form, so all the plant's vigor goes to the edible stalks. The only other thing you have to do is harvest those luscious stalks and eat them. But don't sample the leaves — they're poisonous.

Easy Watering

Do you water frequently? Leave a section of hose laid out down the center of the garden. Drive double stakes of wood at intervals to keep the hose from decimating the vegetables as you pull it back and forth.

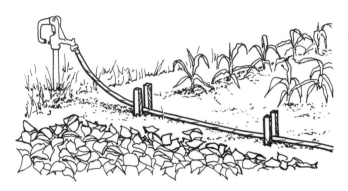

*Double stakes protect your garden from ravages
caused by an unguided hose.*

Another gardener, who has several small vegetable plots, drives a stake at the corner of each bed to protect plants while he drags the hose around.

• • •

Most of us move sprinklers around to get an even watering in a garden area. It takes time, and the water is rarely spread evenly. A neighbor of mine, starting a garden, set up his sprinkler and staked out exactly where it watered. Those were the boundaries of his garden.

• • •

Water the garden with a **soaker hose.** It's easy to install and it makes watering painless thereafter.

• • •

A chrysanthemum in the vegetable garden is like a canary in a coal mine. **The mum wilts before other plants** when water is needed, giving you early warning to start irrigating.

Save your water from cooking vegetables. Let it cool. Toss out the door on the herbs or salad greens in your kitchen garden, or the flowers, if that's what grows there. In winter, use for houseplants.

• • •

Don't be a slave to the water hose. Everyone knows that the best gardens are those that are watered regularly, but hand watering can eat up a lot of time. To remedy this, attach an **electronic timer** to your outdoor garden faucet. They are easy to set, and many run off inexpensive size C batteries. The timers allow the garden to be watered up to eight times a day for just about as long as you want. With this little gadget, you can even water the garden in your sleep.

Don't Forget the Flowers

Plant tiny bulbs such as snowdrops, scilla, crocus, grape hyacinths, and chionodoxa in a place they'll be noticed in early spring but undisturbed during the summer. There's nothing worse than inadvertently digging them up as you cultivate after their foliage has disappeared and you've forgotten they were there. Instead of putting them in a flower bed, try them below light mulch under deciduous trees and shrubs.

• • •

Beware of gifts. If your flower-gardening friends offer pieces of perennials they're dividing, investigate the plant's growing habits before you plunk it in the ground. It may be a spreader that will take over the garden and become a nuisance.

Alternatively, you may wish to plant perennials that spread quickly. Many people avoid the most vigorous plants, such as sneezewort, tawny daylily, and peach-leaf bellflower, because they spread quickly and need almost no care. Sounds like a great garden to me!

• • •

Have you inherited **old flower gardens** with your newly purchased home? "It pays to sit and watch for a year. If something continues to grow despite neglect, it's hardy. Don't fight it, keep it," advises an experienced restorer of old grounds. You may find it easier to relocate gardens using old plant material, rather than trying to refurbish a garden in the same place. You can prepare soil in a new bed and move pieces of plants from the old site when you are ready.

Out, Weeds!

THE EXTREME CASE of the lazy gardener might be the college professor who planted his entire vegetable patch in spring and never looked at it again until it was time to harvest. He overplanted and just let the whole business go weedy. He got enough food for the family out of the enterprise, and that was all he was after in the first place.

Most of us aren't that lazy. We take pride in order and control. The specter of carefully planned and planted crops being choked by weeds makes us shiver. We dream of lush crops and flamboyant flowers with few weeds, but we'd like to be able to reach that goal without accepting slavery. So we compromise and let a few weeds grow, or take a different tack and smother them with mulch.

Beat the Weeds

The secret to weed control, say knowledgeable gardeners, is to **get them while they're little.** Begin cultivation as soon as weeds appear. It's light work to knock them down then; later, when they're firmly rooted and threatening to take over the garden, eliminating them is hard work.

Studies have shown that vegetable gardens that are weeded all season long have about the same yields as gardens weeded until the crops reach fruit set. This means that rather than weed during those last few weeks, gardeners can grow good crops from the lounge chair.

Peter Henderson wrote this in 1901, and it still applies today: "In no work in which men are engaged is the adage, 'A stitch in time saves nine,' more applicable than to the work of the farm or garden. The instant that weeds appear, attack them with the hoe or rake. Do not wait for them to get a foot high, or a twelfth part of it, but break every inch of the surface crust of the ground just as soon as a germ of weed growth shows itself. And it will be better to do it even before any weeds show, for by using a small, sharp steel rake, two or three days after your crop is planted or sown, you will **kill the weeds just as they are germinating.**"

• • •

"Limit the time you spend weeding and **develop a routine,**" suggests Phil Viereck. "It's a favorite morning ritual for me. I take a sharp wide hoe and spend twenty minutes each morning cultivating. I do the garden in pieces. Twenty minutes of a garden a day is so much better than three hours occasionally."

• • •

Want to sail (play golf or tennis, hike, bike, lie in a hammock) in July and August? Weed now and sail later. Skip **spring weeding** and you'll pay all summer. Kit Foster says, "We put in lots of time weeding in spring and the rest of the summer we weed just one day a week."

• • •

"Some people get concerned if there's a weed here and there," says Ray Lambert. "I don't as long as they don't take over the plants. They're part of the garden. I practice **walk-through weeding** in my raised-bed garden. Whenever I walk through, I pull a few of the most insidious weeds."

• • •

After a good rain, when the soil is soft and weed roots give little resistance is the **best time to weed.** Let foliage dry first, to avoid spreading disease.

• • •

An experienced gardener says, "A crop like peas we don't bother to weed much. By the time the weeds are big enough to bother the peas, the harvest is over."

• • •

If weeding isn't your favorite outdoor sport, do what a Charlotte, Vermont, gardener does. "Weed thoroughly and often early in the season, so the vegetables, even the tiny carrots, get a good start. Then, about July 15, when most vegetables are well up, I wish them well, and tell them they're on their own. By that time they're growing ahead of the weeds, and the few weeds that do come up don't interfere with their growth." If he plants fall crops, a late row of lettuce, for example, he'll weed that carefully, just as if it had been started in the spring.

• • •

"When I weed a flower garden," says Nora Stevenson, "I never cart the weeds off in a wheelbarrow. 'All those seeds are just green manure, a source of humus.' I tuck them in the back, behind the flowers, thinly, so they don't mold before they begin to disintegrate."

• • •

Carry a pair of **pliers** as part of your weeding arsenal. Use them to pull out tough weeds, like tree seedings, that won't succumb to a gentle jerk of the hand.

• • •

Another handy tool is a **dandelion-weeder** or daisy grubber — good for tap-rooted plants that can't be pulled easily by hand.

• • •

Try a **hula hoe** or scuffle hoe. Drag it through the garden, and it cuts weeds below the surface of the soil, at the growing point.

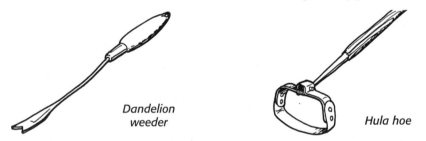

Dandelion
weeder

Hula hoe

Eat the Weeds

A weed, they say, is a plant growing where it's not wanted. Learn to love some of your weeds. Think of them as free vegetables. Don't fight them, eat them!

My asparagus patch bears a luscious crop of early **dandelion greens**, indicators of rich soil. I harvest them with glee before cultivating the bed in early spring. Chopped and tossed in a salad with young scallions, they symbolize all the vigor and strength of a new gardening year.

Use young **purslane** raw in salads, too.

. . .

Lamb's quarters are a delectable spinach substitute. Whenever you spy a baby in your garden, let it grow a bit, then strip leaves off tough stems, steam, and toss with butter. Once you taste lamb's quarters, you'll search for them everywhere.

One day, I parked behind a store in our small town and found a huge crop of them growing next to the building. I began cutting and stuffing the weed into all the empty spaces in my grocery bags. "What are you doing?" asked the curious occupant of a parked car.

"Harvesting my vegetable for supper tonight," I said, giggling, and left him shaking his head in disbelief.

Smother the Weeds with Mulch

The queen of mulch was Ruth Stout, author of *How to Have a Green Thumb Without an Aching Back*. She maintained a year-round hay mulch at least eight inches deep in her Connecticut vegetable garden. In her fifty-by-fifty-foot plot, she used twenty-five bales a year. She never turned the soil, sowed a cover crop, hoed, weeded, watered, or built a compost pile. She just mulched, making compost on the spot, for as the bottom layer of mulch decomposed, it added rich organic matter to the soil — a continuing process. Ruth didn't bother with manures, but used cottonseed meal or soy bean meal for added nitrogen. She sprinkled it on top of the mulch in winter, at a rate of five pounds to one hundred square feet, so that snow and rain carried it down through the hay by planting time. To plant, she pulled aside the mulch and sowed the seed.

. . .

Mulch saves weeding, which should make aficionados of all lazy gardeners. Add to that its other virtues. Mulch:

- Conserves moisture. Mulchers rarely, if ever, water crops.
- Reduces compaction of soil when people walk on it.
- Keeps hard rain from pounding and compacting soil.
- Prevents erosion.
- Keeps dirt from splashing on crops during rains, so you spend less time washing leaf crops after harvest.

- Protects sprawling crops like tomatoes, melons, cucumbers, and squash from direct contact with soil, so there is less chance for rot.
- Helps maintain an even soil temperature — helps it stay cooler during baking summer days and warmer during chilly spring and fall nights.
- Encourages earthworms.
- As it decomposes, mulch improves the tilth and fertility of soil.

In **northern climates,** year-round mulch may not work as well as in moderate and southern zones. Tomatoes, for instance, are unhappy in cold soil. Beans need warm soil for germination. Mulch keeps soil from warming up in early spring. Pull it back in planting areas for heat-loving crops so that the soil can bake for a week or two before planting time.

• • •

Some northern gardeners till or cultivate until the ground warms up, then mulch for the rest of the summer.

• • •

Before you mulch for the first time, **add extra nitrogen** to the soil. As soil organisms decompose the bottom layer of mulch, they use the nearest available nitrogen — robbing it from the soil if necessary. This problem is greatest with mulching materials low in nitrogen, such as sawdust, leaves, wood chips, or ground corn cobs. If your plants begin to look yellow or stunted, that could mean they're starving for a shot of nitrogen. Run out there quickly, manure tea or any high-nitrogen fertilizer in hand (sodium nitrate, urea, calcium nitrate, or lawn fertilizer). Once the mulching process gets under way, you can add new mulch on top of old without worry.

• • •

Make sure your soil is thoroughly damp before applying mulch. Otherwise, you'll be maintaining soil dryness instead of conserving soil moisture.

• • •

Don't be a miser with mulch. **Make it thick** enough so it can do its job of suppressing weeds. Coarse mulches, such as hay or straw need to be eight to twelve inches deep. Finer mulches can be applied more thinly. Something as fine as coffee grounds needs to be only one-half inch thick. When in doubt, add a little extra; it settles more quickly than you think.

It's easier to **spread mulch on your entire garden**, then part it and plant, than it is to wait until crops are up before mulching. If you do it the hard way, you have the tedious work of placing mulch between and around young plants, and that takes a lot more time.

• • •

Save your old **newspapers** — but not the color pages — for mulches. Lay them two or three sheets thick wherever you don't want weeds to grow. The papers will gradually disintegrate, and when they do, just add more. Don't like the looks of them in your garden? Then try laying a thicker layer first — eight or ten sheets — and covering with a thin layer of straw or some other more attractive mulch. This covering will also keep wind from lifting the newspaper.

Or you can control weeds from the beginning of the gardening season by laying a ½-inch thick mulch of newspaper in the garden and flower beds. Cover the newspaper with a layer of bark mulch or pine needles for season-long weed control.

• • •

Get **a head start** on newspaper mulch in winter. As you finish reading today's paper, staple it to yesterday's. Make strips of newspapers as long as a garden row, roll them up and store until spring. When you need mulch, unroll on the garden.

• • •

When I was a young, newly married gardening novice, we lived on the seashore. A violent December storm drove high tides within a few feet of our front door. When the water receded, a huge pile of eelgrass and seaweed ringed our home. Too lazy to cart it away, we raked the debris a few feet closer to the house and stuffed it under foundation plantings. Our shrubs got a bonanza of enriched soil and added trace minerals, and we, by accident, became mulching devotees. We noticed, for the first time, all the piles of free eelgrass sitting at the end of the street and carted it home to hold moisture in our sandy soil.

• • •

Wherever you live, it's worth keeping **year-round mulch** under shrubs and trees to eliminate cultivating and weeding. Shredded bark, wood chips, cocoa bean hulls, pine needles, and leaf mold are all weed-free and pleasing to look at. Under broad-leaved evergreens, use a mulch of cottonseed meal or pine needles to make soil more acid.

Outline the bed with folded newspapers before you add mulch — keeps a neat edge for a longer time.

· · ·

"I laugh when I think of our first garden," says Deirdre Kevorkian. "Spindly was the word for those plants. The garden was three times as big as this one, but we got much less produce." Now she and Eric have raised beds in a modest twelve-foot by twenty-foot garden, framed with jaunty orange marigolds just inside pressure-treated 6" x 6" timbers. In their small patch, they mulch with **grass clippings.** Every time they mow, they add some more. The carrots, beets, spinach, lettuce, beans, broccoli, tomatoes, peppers, cukes, and winter squash are healthy and bug-free. "I haven't weeded yet this year," Deirdre boasts. "It's almost automatic. Plant, mulch, and wait. I love gardens, but I hate the work."

· · ·

Weed haters are alert for non-commercial sources of mulch. "I was jogging through a development one autumn and I met a man raking pine needles," explains a New Hampshire woman. "We began talking, and soon I had a promise of an **annual supply of pine needles** for my acid loving plants (such as blueberries), and I also talked him into organizing his neighbors to save leaves for me. Of course, I offered inducements. Every summer, I give each of them a supply of plastic bags to use for collecting my mulch in the fall, and at Christmas I thank them with candy. Each autumn, I cart away in my utility trailer twenty-two bags of pine needles and forty-four bags of leaves. They love me!"

· · ·

Hay is a wonderful mulch for vegetables. Bales of hay separate easily into "slices" that can be laid on soil between rows. Don't worry about the weed seeds that sprout from the hay itself. Simply lay more hay on top, or roll it over. Hay transforms soil into black, fluffy loam.

MULCHING MATERIALS — FROM HAY TO Z

Be imaginative in collecting mulching materials. Buy if you must, or scavenge from friends or local industries. (Be sure to add nitrogen where noted.) Try:

hay (a farmer might be delighted to unload spoiled bales)

straw

leaves (shred or rotary mow first)

hulls or shells from cocoa beans, buckwheat, peanuts, rice, cottonseed, oats, or nuts

grass clippings (ask your neighbors or a lawn-maintenance service to save them)

wood chips (get them from a utility company pruning near overhead wires) (add nitrogen)

shredded bark (add nitrogen)

sawdust (add nitrogen)

seaweed, kelp, eelgrass

ground corn cobs and stalks (add nitrogen)

shredded sugar cane

packing materials (excelsior, shredded paper)

salt hay

coffee grounds

partly finished compost

pebbles

ground oyster shells

newspaper

peat moss (it cakes, is really better dug into soil)

Spanish moss

tobacco stems (but keep them away from tomatoes, peppers, eggplant, and potatoes)

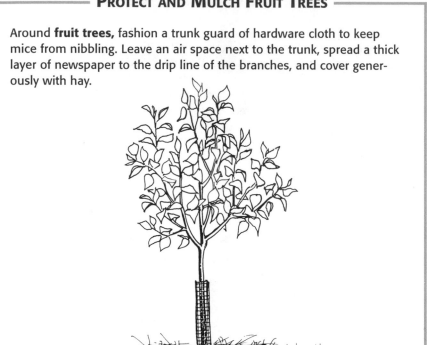

Around **fruit trees,** fashion a trunk guard of hardware cloth to keep mice from nibbling. Leave an air space next to the trunk, spread a thick layer of newspaper to the drip line of the branches, and cover generously with hay.

If you mulch your strawberries with **grain straw,** you could be planting trouble. The seeds will reach the ground and grow like weeds. Avoid this trouble by breaking open the bales and wetting them so all seeds will sprout before the mulch is used.

• • •

If you raise **blueberries,** you know the chore that weeding around them can be. A little work in September will save you hours of work next spring and summer. Mulch the bushes with ground pine bark, pine needles, or well-rotted sawdust. Spread mulch at least four inches deep, so that it will be at least two inches deep when it settles.

• • •

Peppers respond best to dark-colored mulches.

• • •

Carrots love coffee grounds, applied sparingly. Add a touch of lime to offset acidity.

Try Black Plastic

"Black plastic has freed me from hours of weeding. I never used to finish that chore," explains a Massachusetts gardener. "I resisted black plastic because it looks so awful, but we put dirt along the edges and scatter some on top, and that helps. We use three-foot-wide rolls in our entire vegetable garden. We plant a row, lay the plastic, anchor the edges with dirt, plant another row, and so on. The weeding always had hung over me. Now I just hand-weed in the row itself, and we have more time to canoe or play tennis."

• • •

Do your muskmelons sometimes taste like squash? **For increased sweetness,** plant through black plastic. It will heat up the soil several degrees, and that often makes the difference between tasteless and first-rate melons.

• • •

"I can't bear to put holes in my beautiful 6-mil black plastic," says one lazy gardener. In April, she rototills, fertilizes, and digs organic matter into the plot where she plans to plant heat-loving crops. She lays large sheets of 6-mil black plastic over the soil and leaves them to kill weeds and heat soil until planting time in late May or early June. She lifts the plastic and carefully stores it, whole instead of holey, until next year; then she plants melons, cucumbers,and other **heat-loving crops** in warm, weedless soil, and lays "cheap black plastic" (1.5 mil) around them for continuing easy maintenance.

• • •

Warning: If you have snakes in your area, they may find the extra heat under the black plastic inviting and crawl under it. Beware!

The Weed-Free Asparagus Bed

"Please, please tell me how to keep weeds out of the asparagus patch," pleaded one frustrated gardener.

"My Dad had the **ideal solution** for weeds in his asparagus patch," a grower explains. "He built a fence around the bed, and after the harvest, when the spears had grown up tall and lacy, let his chickens loose inside the fence. They ate all the weeds, kept the asparagus beetle under control and fertilized the soil with their droppings"

Plant **annual ryegrass** in the asparagus bed after the last harvest in spring. It crowds out other weeds in summer, and dies in the winter. Next spring you'll have mulch already in place, and it won't interfere with emerging spears.

• • •

Cultivate the patch in early spring, two or three weeks before spears emerge, weed once after cutting, and mulch heavily for the rest of summer. One gardener saves his grass clippings for mulch, since they're weed-free.

• • •

The Ruth Stout way is to **keep the asparagus bed heavily mulched.** Each fall, add eight inches of loose hay. In winter, broadcast cotton-seed meal and wood ashes on the mulch. The soil warms more slowly in spring, but the hay also protects the asparagus from tip-kill by late frosts. If you can't wait for those delectable spears, push the mulch aside in spring. Or split the harvest, by removing mulch from half the bed for an early crop.

A Few Final Weed-Beating Ideas

Weeds in **perennial flower beds** are the gardener's nemesis. How do you enrich the soil and mulch it without introducing weed seeds? "I have a new system that works," says Closey Dickey. "Never, never again will I add horse manure, and I'm loathe even to use compost. Instead, I topdress every fall with a mixture of peat moss, bone meal, dried cow manure [no weed seeds], and churned-up leaves."

• • •

Weeds are always a nuisance among **onions and garlic.** A fine, weed-free mulch, such as peat moss or grass clippings, applied soon after planting will lick the problem. You'll have less area to mulch if you plant in wide rows or square beds.

• • •

Can't be bothered with mulches?

- One gardener sets his lawnmower high and mows weekly between his garden rows, forming weed paths between the vegetables.

• Another says, "To have a good garden, you have to get down on your knees once in a while. Recently, I've found it pretty difficult to do that. [The speaker is in his mid-eighties.] So I leave four feet between rows and use my rototiller regularly to maintain a dust mulch and keep weeds down. It's a waste of land, but it makes it possible for me to keep a garden."

To **lick weeds,** concentrate for just one year. This approach works particularly well on areas that haven't been gardened before, but may be full of weed seeds. In the spring, till, then **plant buckwheat** at the rate of four pounds per thousand square feet. This is heavy seeding. After it has blossomed, but before the dark seeds form, till the buckwheat under. A day later, plant another crop of buckwheat, again four pounds per thousand square feet. Again, the buckwheat will come up, and so, too, will the weeds, but the buckwheat again will outgrow and eventually kill off the weeds by shading them out. This time, be particularly sure the seed hasn't formed before you till it, or the buckwheat will be the weed you're faced with next year.

A Scythe

If weeds are growing around the perimeter of your garden, scattering seeds into the garden, cut those weeds with a scythe, then add them to the compost pile. A scythe is a remarkably efficient tool in the hands of an expert. Don't flail at weeds with a scythe. Hold it loosely, comfortably, and move the blade by pivoting your body, keeping the blade parallel to and close to the ground. Stop often to sharpen the blade. A scythe doesn't get dull very quickly, but frequent sharpening is a good way to relax shoulder and arm muscles.

After tilling in the second crop of buckwheat, plant another cover crop, such as annual ryegrass or winter rye. The result will be three cover crops tilled into the soil, enriching it, plus almost all the weeds eliminated from the site. This is an excellent method to use before raising strawberries since weeds are what usually do in a bed of them.

• • •

Has your soil been poisoned with herbicides? This could be the case on a lawn that you now want to turn into a flower or vegetable garden. It could take as long as five years for the residue to dissipate. You can speed the process by adding extra organic matter to the soil and deep-watering to wash residues away. If the contamination is bad, you may want to mix activated charcoal with the soil, at a rate of 300 pounds per acre.

• • •

If you are tired of trying to weed between stepping stones and sidewalks, the Primus Weed Torch is for you. This tool kills weeds with a regulated flame. It is fast, easy, and you don't even have to bend over.

Pests and Pestilence

HERE'S WHERE the proverbial ounce of prevention is worth a pound of cure. Once the woodchuck has chopped off your beans at ground level, the raccoon has stripped and devoured every ear of corn, and the cucumber beetles have decimated emerging seedlings, you may as well throw up your hands in surrender and hightail it to the nearest farmer's market with wallet in hand.

Recall the lazy gardener's goal and build your soil for fertility and tilth. Insects and diseases do the most damage on unhealthy plants. Robust plants draw their vigor from soil. Check yours for proper pH and sufficient nutrients, keep its organic content high, make sure there's enough water by irritating and mulching, control weeds while plants are little, and rotate crops.

Read the blurbs in seed catalogs to find disease-resistant varieties, choose seeds adapted to your geographic area, and grow plants in season.

Varmints Spell Trouble

Fence Defense

"The woodchuck got to me. He ate EVERYTHING — an entire row of beans in one night. I couldn't feed him and me, too."

If you're in a country place where the woodchuck and rabbit populations are high, **you need a fence.** Invest some time and effort to construct one that's burrow-proof. Do it in fall, while the memory of crops unsavored (because the varmint got there first) still stings.

BURROW-PROOF AND NIBBLE-PROOF

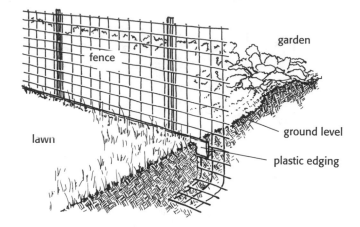

Friends of mine marshalled their strong sons to install a fence that is 3 feet above ground (stretched on metal fence post(s), 1 foot below ground, and runs 1 foot out horizontally, underground, to discourage burrowing beasts.

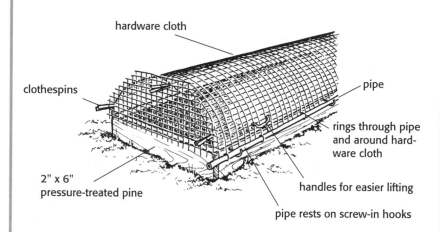

Cover your raised salad bed to make it nibble-proof. Rig a tunnel of hardware cloth to protect lettuce, spinach, basil, and parsley grown in the bed. Staple the hardware cloth on one side. Attach a pipe to the other side to weigh it down. The pipe rests on hooks screwed into the pressure-treated pine timbers that contain the bed. Handles above the pipes make it easy to lift the mesh to cultivate and harvest. To close in the ends, attach pieces of hardware cloth with clothespins.

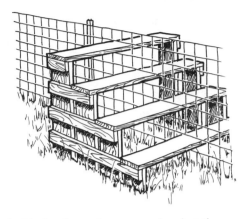

STILE FOR FOOT TRAFFIC

If you've decided to fence in your garden, but the creation of a gate sounds technical, consider a **stile.** It's easy to build, offers a place to put things, and makes an easy entrance to the garden. But don't try to run a tiller up over the top!

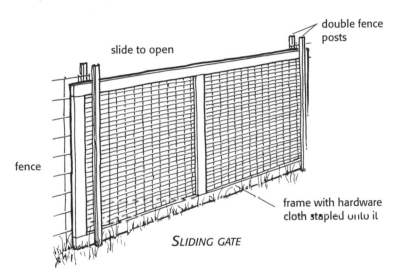

double fence posts

slide to open

fence

frame with hardware cloth stapled onto it

SLIDING GATE

If you till, you'll need a fence opening wide enough for garden machinery. Gates can be complicated to construct. Bob and Eleanor Kolkebeck have devised a simple substitute. On each side of their 5½-foot wide fence openings, they drove two metal fence posts (leaving four feet extending above ground) so there is a slot between them. The gate is a 3- by 6-foot wooden frame with hardware cloth stretched on it. It slides between the double fence posts like a sliding door — no hinges or latches to fuss with. Just remember to close it when you leave the garden!

Tactics for the Truly Lazy

A four-foot fence won't stop deer from entering your garden? Don't believe it! Lay **four-foot wide chicken wire** horizontally around the perimeter of the garden. Deer won't walk on it. Stake it down so that it lies fairly loosely on the ground.

• • •

The **family cat** prowling the garden will control its population of chipmunks, mice, and young rabbits.

• • •

Cut plastic gallon milk jugs in half lengthwise. Punch a hole in the bottom to let out rain. Set ripening melons in these contraptions. They help **prevent rot** and keep mice and shrews from nibbling on the melons.

• • •

Are rodents feasting on your tulip bulbs? Plant daffodils instead. Their bulbs are bitter, so mice and chipmunks won't eat them.

If you're determined to have **tulips,** interplant with *Frittilaria imperialis* bulbs. The two- to three-foot tall plants have pendulous red, orange, or yellow blooms. They exude a skunk-like odor that repels rodents and moles.

• • •

A house wren feeds 500 bugs and caterpillars to her babies in one afternoon; a brown thrasher consumes thousands of bugs a day. Spot some simple bird baths here and there in your garden as enticement to **feathered helpers.** Fill large terra cotta saucers, the ones made for placing under flower pots, with water, and set on logs turned on end.

• • •

Save **fur** from brushing and grooming your dog. Scatter it in the garden. It deters nibblers and also adds nitrogen to the soil as it decomposes. No dog? Ask the local pet-grooming operation to save fur for you, or try human hair from the barbershop.

• • •

Birds are welcome if they're eating the bugs, but do you want them to snitch your berries? Actually, I think it's rather fun to share my raspberries. I enjoy having the catbird perch atop a bean pole, tail switching, emitting scolding sounds as I pick her red jewels. There are always enough berries left for me. If your generosity doesn't match mine, cover your berry bushes and strawberry beds with used **tobacco netting** as the fruit begins to ripen. It can be easily lifted when you want to harvest.

Why should you do all the hard work of getting rid of unwanted insects? Get some help on the job. Make a few **birdhouses** like this one, place them near the garden, and the birds will pitch in hungrily.

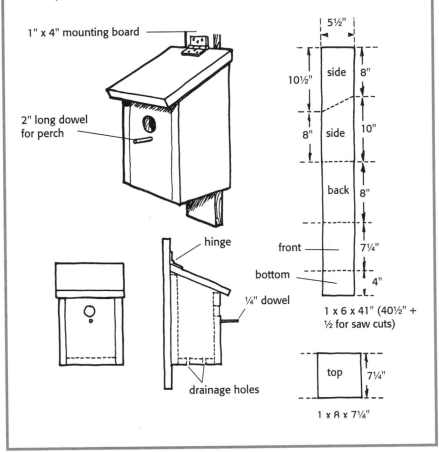

1" x 4" mounting board

2" long dowel for perch

hinge

¼" dowel

drainage holes

5½"

side   8"

10½"

8"   side   10"

back   8"

front   7¼"

bottom   4"

1 x 6 x 41" (40½" + ½ for saw cuts)

top   7¼"

1 x 8 x 7¼"

A clever gardener replaces the windows of portable cold frames with screens and sets them over ripening strawberry plants to keep out the birds.

• • •

Plant for the birds, and they'll be less likely to raid cultivated berries. They prefer the tartness of wild fruit, so nurture red and black chokeberry, barberry, wild honeysuckle, autumn olive, Russian olive, mountain ash, staghorn sumac, and mulberry. Barberry and wild honeysuckle can be quite invasive once getting a foothold, so plant wisely.

Keep **ravenous crows** from pulling up newly planted corn. Scatter crow repellent, available at seed stores, on the bed, or mulch loosely with hay after seeding.

• • •

I take a tip from Jim Brady. He realized that his corn growing was for the birds — they got every seedling that came up — so he tried something different. He laid down a three-foot wide strip of **black plastic,** cut holes in it, then planted the corn through the holes. The birds stayed away from the corn. "They just didn't like walking on that plastic," he explained. He's getting a couple of other benefits from the plastic. The soil is warmer, which speeds the growth of the corn, and there's no weeding, which he misses not one bit.

FOIL THE BIRDS

"One year, the birds took one peck out of each ripening tomato and then it would rot. It infuriated me," explains a Massachusetts gardener who now takes some time to "foil" the birds. She and her husband have drilled a hole through the top of each six-foot high tomato stake, and after the stakes are in the ground, they thread twine loosely from stake to stake. Halfway between stakes, they hang four-inch diameter aluminum pie plates. The pie plates must be put up at the same time the tomatoes are planted, not after the birds start eating.

Coons and Corn

Raccoons have an unmatched affinity for ripening corn. I talked with only one gardener who had no problem with raccoon-ravaged sweet corn. His garden is bordered by a pasture. The cows keep the grass cropped and coons and woodchucks won't cross the large, open expanse to raid the corn.

Most of us aren't that lucky. We don't feel like lazy gardeners when all of our work goes to feeding raccoons, squirrels, and woodchucks. Maybe one, or a combination of, these antidotes for varmints in the corn patch will work for you:

- Put a strand or two of electric fencing around the garden, one six inches above the ground the other fifteen inches high.
- Cover almost-ripe ears with a paper bag and secure with a twistem.
- Keep a transistor radio playing at night in the corn patch. Stick it in a plastic bag as protection against rain.
- Interplant corn with large-leaved pumpkins and squash. Supposedly raccoons and squirrels don't like to walk on the leaves.
- Surround early corn with a double row of late corn. Hope the raccoons will think none of the patch is yet ripe, while you feast on the early harvest.
- Add a floppy overhang of chicken wire, about two feet wide, to the top of your garden fence. It won't support the weight of animals that try to climb over.

Bugs and Diseases

Lazy gardeners are willing to let a few bugs eat. "I simply plant too much," says one gardener. "I give my crops rich soil and let them fend for themselves. There are all kinds of bugs, and I don't have time to fool with them, so if they eat half my chard, I eat the other half."

• • •

"Most gardeners panic when they see one bug eating," says another gardener, who chides the "spray-happy people who rain destruction on a whole garden for one squash bug. I usually let them eat, and spray only when a crop is really threatened." Insect pests will eventually come into balance with their natural enemies, he suggests.

So encourage the population of **beneficial creatures** such as birds, bats, toads, snakes, spiders, ladybugs, and the praying mantis. They'll eat lots of those pesky bugs, and you'll have more time for summer fun.

• • •

There's a gardener in a town near Toledo, Ohio, who has a mean tennis backhand. During garden season, he's out there practicing it. His targets are those white butterflies that dance over the cabbages and other members of the cabbage family. Eventually, unless he swats them, they land, lay eggs, and from those eggs emerge the hungry **cabbage loopers.** One of those dainty butterflies can lay as many as 300 eggs, and 299 of them may hatch. There's a better, less tiring way of halting the life cycle of those loopers. It's called *Bacillus thuringiensis,* or BT; or commercially, Dipel, Biotrol, and Thuricide. It's so effective that you can eat broccoli without wondering about trace amounts of toxins, and it's pure enough even for the most committed organic gardener. Spray about once a week during the early weeks of the season, or mix it in a watering can (one tablespoon to four gallons of water) and sprinkle on the plant. Try it if you haven't; you'll never practice that backhand in the garden again — or use some of the less desirable sprays.

• • •

If **ground-nesting hornets** decide to nest near the garden, watch them carefully from a distance to determine the exact site of the entrance hole. At night, when the hornets have retreated inside the nest, fill a long-necked beer bottle half full of gasoline. Carefully approach the nest, and stick the bottle neck first into the entrance hole. Leave the bottle in place for one week.

• • •

In warm regions, you can reduce cockroach problems by **removing foundation plantings.** Foundation plantings are prime cockroach habitat. Replace them with stone mulch around the house to reduce cockroach populations.

Get Tough with Slugs

Slugs — hazards in a mulched garden or in damp soil — especially love new seedlings. If you can't say with aplomb, as does one lazy gardener, "There's plenty for the slugs and me," what can you do?

- Slugs can't tolerate sharp or **caustic materials** against their soft bodies. Spread a half-inch deep, six-inch diameter circle of sharp sand around new seedings, or try wood ashes, lime, cinders, or diatomaceous earth.
- Give them a **beer** party. One former school teacher pours beer into shallow dishes and spots them in her garden for slug bait.
- Feeling murderous? Stalk slugs in evening with a salt shaker. Sprinkle them twice for insurance. Or fill a spray bottle with a solution of half-water, half-vinegar and spray on slugs.
- Put shingles in the garden as traps. Each morning, lift the shingles and kill the slugs gathered there.

Cutworms and Other Annoyances

No lazy gardener wants to replace transplants severed at ground level by **cutworms**. Protect yours with collars pushed one inch into the ground. Make them from:

- Tin cans with top and bottom removed,
- Paper cups with bottoms punched out,
- Sections of milk cartons,
- Cardboard,
- A two-inch square of two thicknesses of newspaper placed around each stem.

That shovelful of compost thrown in a planting hole helps **protect transplants** against insect attack. If a transplant is put in poor soil, it develops more carbohydrates and less protein than normal. Insects crave carbohydrates, so they flock to the poorly nourished plant.

• • •

Blossom end-rot on tomatoes is caused by lack of calcium. If you're sure there's enough lime in your soil, it may be a lack of even moisture that is making the calcium unavailable to the plant. Prevent this by mulching and keep lots of organic matter in the soil.

• • •

Do you need the shade of a beach umbrella at the seashore to keep from scorching? Like you, tomatoes need protection from the sun. Be a little lazy and don't prune them too severely. To **prevent sunscald**, they need those leaves to shade their fruit.

For a lazy gardener's attack against root knot nematodes (most prevalent in the South), plant lots of **French marigolds,** whose roots exude a repellent, and keep the soil extra high in organic matter. Beneficial fungi that grow in decomposing humus keep these pests under control.

. . .

Hill earth over **carrots** to prevent a pesky fly from laying eggs in the top of the carrot root.

. . .

Let us have light — and **scare away the aphids,** which are accustomed to the cool, dark undersides of leaves. Spread a square of aluminum foil under affected plants. Supposedly, the aphids are confused by the increased light and leave. Do this around squash plants, too, to repel the squash bug. If you don't get rid of the bugs, the foil will at least act as mulch to smother weeds and will bounce more light on crops that need much sun.

. . .

If **green lacewings** invade your garden, do nothing but welcome them. Their larvae are death to aphids.

. . .

Know and control your soil's pH. **Keep it sweet** — almost at 7.0 — and you'll discourage club root disease in cabbages, broccoli, cauliflower, and the rest of the brassicas. Keep scab off potatoes with an acid soil — below 5 or an alkaline soil — 7 or above. Scab is worst when the pH is around 6.

. . .

Plant **white radishes with cucumbers** to deter cucumber beetles.

. . .

Tired of growing roses just so bugs and diseases have a place to stay? Grow **species roses** instead. Most are carefree and beautiful.

Sayonara, Japanese Beetles

Hire your children to save the garden from **Japanese beetles.** Pay them a penny a bug. In the evening, when the beetles won't fly away, the kids can tiptoe along and brush them from plant foliage into jars of kerosene. Bet they won't even be able to count their catch! Meanwhile, you can relax with a long novel or take in the evening news.

If Japanese beetle grubs are destroying your **lawn,** introduce milky spore disease, a microbial attack against the larval form of this insect. A little energy invested this year is well spent. Put a teaspoon in the ground every three feet for several years' protection. It's death to the grubs, but leaves the earthworm population untouched.

• • •

Cheer when you see little round nose-holes in your lawn. They're a sign **the resident skunk** has been feasting at night, ferreting out grubs. What could be better than volunteer pest control while you sleep?

• • •

Let a bug trap do all the work for you. It entices Japanese beetles with **a female sex scent** combined with a floral lure. Victims are trapped in a bag and die inside from sun's heat. Replace the bag when it's full. One trap services 5,000 square feet. Be sure to hang it thirty feet downwind of plants you want to protect. If you set it near the plants, it will attract beetles to them.

A Dozen Clever Tricks

1. A drop of **mineral oil on corn silk** will keep out worms. Apply to tip of each ear when silks begin to brown, with a medicine dropper, pump-type oil can with a long spout, or a plastic dish-washing detergent bottle. Do it a total of about three times, once every five or six days. What's lazy about this, you wonder? When you harvest the corn, most of the silk will come off with the husk — for worm-free and silk-free ears.

2. If you can prevent plant disease with **good cultural practices,** then you'll never need to use extra time to fight them:

- Immediately after a rain when plants are still wet, rest. That way, you won't be in the garden, brushing up against plants and possibly spreading disease.
- Locate plants where they'll have good air circulation and plenty of sunlight.
- Mulch. It not only saves weeding and watering, but prevents soil-borne diseases from being spread to plants by mud splashed up during rainstorms.
- Don't throw diseased plant material into the compost pile.

- If you're pruning fruit trees for fire blight, take an extra minute to dip your pruning tool into bleach before each cut and burn infested twigs afterward.
- Practice good sanitation. Under roses, for instance, rake up all old rose leaves in fall and spring. They harbor black spot and other fungus diseases.

3. To **control mildew,** make a batch of chamomile tea using pure chamomile. Pour the cooled tea into a spray bottle and use on plants such as rosemary and sage to control mildew. Avoid spraying when plants are in direct sun.

4. If **early blight** is a problem for your tomatoes, plant the heirloom, "potato-leaf" varieties in the spring. These tomatoes are naturally resistant to early blight and will save you from replanting the tomato patch.

5. **Scarecrows** were the original remote control way to protect the garden. The latest improvement on the scarecrow idea is the Terror-eyes balloon; a fifteen-inch beachball decorated with huge eye designs. The balloon is suspended from a pole on a string and allowed to float free in the breeze. As the balloon moves in the breeze the scary eyes frighten marauding birds away, and you don't even break a sweat.

6. Many gardens are magnets to insect pests and controlling them once meant time-consuming patrols through the garden spraying or hand-picking bugs. New **repellents made of garlic oil** can dramatically reduce the bug problems in the garden. Simply spray the product on the crops. The spray does not change the taste of vegetables and quickly becomes odorless to people, but it repels mites, aphids, leaf-rollers, and many more insects for days.

7. Dividing rhizomes or tubers of flowering perennials? Dust the cut part with **sulfur** to prevent rotting.

8. The usual antidote for **mealybugs** on houseplants is to swab each one painstakingly with a Q-tip dipped in alcohol. Save time and

energy. Screw a recycled spray top into the alcohol bottle and spray directly.

9. "I forget white fly, aphids and all those other things on my house-plants," says a prolific grower. "Many people are more meticulous than I. I don't mind bugs. If the infestation gets bad, I never get out the poison sprays. I fill a container with water and **a little soap** and submerge the whole plant for twenty-four hours."

10. **Aphids flock to yellow.** Fill a yellow dishpan part way with water and set in the garden. Aphids will land on the water and be trapped. They drown and sink.

11. If **fire ants** plague you Southern gardeners, pour one inch of Epsom salts in and around their homes.

12. When insects do get ahead of your plants, you'll upset natural balances least if you use a botanically derived insecticide. **Rotenone,** which comes from the roots of two tropical plants, derris and cube, has a drawback. Alas, it kills ladybug larvae as well as the bad guys. **Pyrethrum,** made from the dried flowers of chrysanthemums, spares ladybugs and bees.

Don't Coddle Moths — Protect Fruit Trees

Protect fruit trees from snails by surrounding their trunks with a three-inch wide collar of **copper sheeting,** one foot above the ground.

• • •

Lazy gardeners plan ahead. Control next summer's **codling moth** infestation of apple trees. This year, in July, apply a sticky barrier of tanglefoot to apple tree trunks. It will trap codling moth larvae, thereby cutting the population of moths next year.

Catch the ones you missed by hanging a can or two of bait in each tree when apples first begin to develop. Make it with nine parts water, one part molasses, one part honey, and a little yeast. Change weekly for six weeks.

When you're itching to plant, but planting season isn't here yet, use some of that extra energy to spray **dormant fruit trees** with miscible oil. In early spring, insects that hatch from eggs laid the previous fall are vulnerable because their egg cases and the protective covering of hibernating scales become more porous and allow the spray to penetrate. It covers the potential pests with a film of oil, which suffocate them. Make sure to do this before any buds open.

•   •   •

Take a few minutes to **clean up the spring** drop from fruit trees to help prevent disease and insect infestation.

Companion Planting

Herbs are easy to grow and a boon to the gardener who'd just as soon have someone or something else do pest control. Interplant crops with onions, garlic, and marigolds. Try sage, mint, catnip, or dill among your cabbages. Sage, for instance, gives off camphor, which repels the cabbage butterfly. Herbs may discourage insect infestation not only by their specific effects, but by breaking up a large planting of one crop, which is an open invitation to pests.

COMPANIONABLE HERBS

HERB	COMPANIONS
Basil	Companion to tomatoes; *dislikes* rue. Repels flies and mosquitoes.
Borage	Companion to tomatoes, squash, and strawberries; deters tomato worm.
Caraway	Plant here and there; loosens soil.
Catnip	Plant in borders; deters flea beetle.
Chamomile	Companion to cabbages and onions
Chervil	Companion to radishes.
Chives	Companion to carrots.
Dead Nettle	Companion to potatoes; deters potato bug.
Dill	Companion to cabbage; *dislikes* carrots.

We'd love your thoughts...

Your reactions, criticisms, things you did or didn't like about this Storey Book. Please use space below (or write a letter if you'd prefer — even send photos!) telling how you've made use of the information . . . how you've put it to work . . . the more details the better! Thanks in advance for your help in building our library of good Storey Books.

Pamela B. Art

Publisher

Book Title: _____

Purchased From: _____

Comments: _____

_____

_____

_____

_____

_____

Your Name: _____

Address: _____

☐ Please check here if you'd like our latest Storey's *Books for Country Living* Catalog.

☐ You have my permission to quote from my comments, and use these quotations in ads, brochures, mail, and other promotions used to market your books.

Signed _____ Date _____

email=Feedback@Storey.Com

HERB	COMPANIONS
Fennel	*Most plants dislike it;* plant away from gardens.
Flax	Companion to carrots, potatoes; deters potato bug.
Garlic	Plant near roses and raspberries; deters Japanese beetle.
Horseradish	Plant at corners of potato patch; deters potato bug.
Henbit	General insect repellent.
Hyssop	Companion to cabbage and grapes; deters cabbage moth. *Dislikes* radishes.
Marigolds	Plant throughout garden; it discourages Mexican bean beetles, nematodes, and other insects. The workhorse of companion plants.
Mint	Companion to cabbage and tomatoes; deters white cabbage moth.
Mole Plant	Deters moles and mice if planted around garden.
Nasturtium	Companion to radishes, cabbage, and cucurbits; plant under fruit trees. Deters aphids, squash bugs, striped pumpkin beetles.
Petunia	Companion to beans.
Pot Marigold	Companion to tomatoes, but plant elsewhere, too. Deters tomato worm, asparagus beetles, and other pests.
Rosemary	Companion to cabbage, beans, carrots, and sage; deters cabbage moth, bean beetles, and carrot fly.
Rue	Companion to roses and raspberries; deters Japanese beetles. *Dislikes* sweet basil.
Sage	Plant with rosemary, cabbage, and carrots; *dislikes* cucumbers. Deters cabbage moth, carrot fly.
Southernwood	Companion to cabbage; deters cabbage moth.
Sowthistle	In moderate amounts, this weed can help tomatoes, onions, and corn.
Summer Savory	Companion to beans and onions; deters bean beetles.
Tansy	Plant under fruit trees; companion to roses and raspberries. Deters flying insects, Japanese beetles, striped cucumber beetles, squash bugs, and ants.
Thyme	Companion to cabbage; deters cabbage worm.
Wormwood	As a borer, it keeps animals from the garden.
Yarrow	Plant along borers, paths, and near aromatic herbs; enhances production of essential oils.

PLANT	INSECT DETERRED
Asters	Most insects
Basil	Flies and mosquitoes
Borage	Tomato worm — improves growth and flavor of tomatoes
Calendula	Most insects
Catnip	Flea beetle
Celery	White cabbage butterfly
Chrysanthemum	Most insects
Dead Nettle	Potato bug — improves growth and flavor of potatoes
Eggplant	Colorado potato beetle
Flax	Potato bug
Garlic	Japanese beetle, other insects, and blight
Geranium	Most insects
Horseradish	Plant at corners of potato patch to deter potato bug
Henbit	General insect repellent
Hyssop	Cabbage moth
Marigold	The workhorse of the pest deterrents. Plant throughout garden to discourage Mexican bean beetles, nematodes, and other insects
Mint	White cabbage moth and ants
Mole Plant	Moles and mice if planted here and there
Nasturtium	Aphids, squash bugs, striped pumpkin beetles
Onion family	Most pests
Petunia	Protects beans
Pot Marigold	Asparagus beetles, tomato worms, and general garden pests
Peppermint	Planted among cabbages, it repels the white cabbage butterfly
Radish	Cucumber beetle, in particular
Rosemary	Cabbage moth, bean beetle, and carrot fly
Rue	Japanese beetle
Sage	Cabbage moth, carrot fly
Salsify	Carrot fly
Southernwood	Cabbage moth

PLANT	INSECT DETERRED
Summer Savory	Bean beetles
Tansy	Flying insects, Japanese beetles, striped cucumber beetles, squash bugs, ants
Tomato	Asparagus beetle
Thyme	Cabbage worm
Wormwood	Carrot fly, white cabbage butterfly, black flea beetle

Source: *Gardening Answers,* Editors of Garden Way Publishing

Harvesting and More

CAN ANYTHING EQUAL THE CRUNCH of freshly picked and barely cooked young snap beans, the sweetness of peas and corn rushed from garden to pot, or the wonder of a sun-ripened tomato? Memories of the goodness of home-grown produce are what prompted my sons to plead for three vegetables a night when they returned from college for their first vacation. Institutional cooking made them realize that the quality of garden-fresh crops is incomparable.

We rejoice in the quality of garden-fresh crops, but there are times when we have been overburdened with their quantity. Is there any among us who hasn't wished for a hammock or a cool splash in the ocean instead of the endless row of ripe raspberries screaming to be picked right now, always on the hottest July day? And did you ever wonder, as I have, why, by the time you picked to the end of the row, more berries had ripened at the beginning? I sometimes think a sorceress rules the ripening of raspberries.

Has the nightmare of being buried in a mountain of unshelled peas invaded your sleep? Or that of zucchini grown larger than the dog, larger than your child, too large even to cart to the compost pile?

One of my gardening friends quips, "I don't like to harvest. I just like to grow." At least once during each season, most of us share that sentiment.

Pick Early, Pick Often

"The best solution to tedious harvesting chores," says a lazy gardener, "is to have lots of kids! Corral them to shell the peas, cut the beans, husk the corn, and skin the beets." Family bees can be fun.

· · ·

But, alas, the kids grow up. Lacking a crew of children, plan a social occasion to mesh with the height of raspberry, pea, or bean season. Bill it as a **harvesting party,** and have a gay time with picking, shelling, and freezing in the same way that folks had with husking bees in times past. It works best with friends who have no garden.

· · ·

Get them while they're little! This time we mean crops, not weeds. It's not only less work to **pick young crops,** they plain taste better than tough, overmature produce. Regular picking encourages a plant to produce more, so you'll have a better harvest. Small, tender vegetables also take less time and energy to process. Keep the joy in gardening — never give growing time for a stringy bean, a seedy cucumber or zucchini, starchy peas or corn, a woody beet, bitter lettuce, or tough spinach.

· · ·

In early spring, when you crave fresh vegetables, you can fool around with cloches and fight frosts and cold earth to strive for unnaturally early crops, or you can raid the perennial flower garden and the woods for an **easy early harvest.**

- Cut **daylily sprouts** when they are about three inches high, steam, drizzle with butter, and serve like asparagus.
- Grab a knife and rush out to your ground cover of **violets** as soon as young leaves form, but before flowers bloom. Cut a batch to steam and eat, tossed with a bit of butter. They're a green of incredible delicacy, a cross in flavor between spinach and asparagus. Just be sure to get them while they're young!
- When the **violets** bloom, put a few in your salad, for color and vitamin C.
- Lucky you, if ostrich fern bedecks your yard. Be alert for emerging **fiddleheads** and snap them off when tightly curled and no more than six inches high. (When taller, they are not safe to eat. In fact, they are poisonous once unfurled.) Don't

remove more than a third to a half of the shoots from any one plant. Pull each stalk through your fingers to remove the felt-like covering and wash quickly in cold water. Eat raw in salads, steam like asparagus, make fiddlehead soup, or blanch for two minutes and freeze for a mid-winter treat. (If none grow in your yard, a likely place to find them is a silty flood plain near a river bed.)

- Leeks in the garden take 120 or more days to mature. For a spring treat without the waiting, enjoy the pungent sharpness of their cousins, the **wild leeks,** found on an early walk in rich woods. Their foliage begins as a tightly curled cylinder, then unfurls to resemble lily-of-the-valley leaves. Chop and add to salads or use for leek soup.

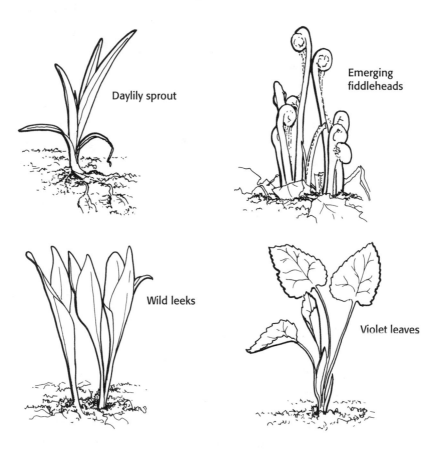

Daylily sprout

Emerging fiddleheads

Wild leeks

Violet leaves

Look for these perennials for an easy, tasty, early harvest.

Here's a simple way to make sure you'll harvest your vegetables when you want them. You can determine the harvest date using the days from planting to harvest listed on seed packets. Put all your vegetables on one chart (see the sample below — be sure to include specific dates!), and you'll be able to time your produce for such uses as spaghetti sauce, which requires more than one vegetable.

Vegetable	April	May	June	July	August
Alaska Peas	✔		•		
Goldie Corn		✔			•
Silver Cross corn		✔			•

✔ Date Planted
• Harvest Period

* * *

Pick fruits and vegetables **in the early morning** when the temperature is cool. To keep them juicy but firm, store in the refrigerator for a hour or so before washing in cool water.

* * *

Bush beans all come at once and picking can be a back-breaking chore. **Save your back** and extend the harvest for a longer time by choosing pole beans instead. Kentucky Wonder or Romano Italian Pole are delectable steamed when young. If you tire of fresh beans or you go on vacation, let the pods mature and use them as shell beans, either immediately or dried for winter meals.

* * *

"I never bend over to **pick bush beans**," John Page says. He explains that, since most of the beans come at once, particularly in determinate varieties, there's no sense in courting a backache simply because you hope to get the few beans that will appear after the main picking. "Just pull out the bean plant, take off all the beans while you're standing up, and throw the plant in the compost." Have a second planting under way for another harvest.

* * *

If you don't want to bother with supports for pole beans, but you'd like to **extend the harvest** for bush beans, choose varieties that produce over a longer period of time: Royal Burgundy, Bush Blue Blake, Cherokee Wax, Eagle, Black Valentine, or Contender.

Thin fruit trees in spring, so fruits are six to ten inches apart. Trees will produce larger fruit, will have less damage from worms, and will set more fruit next year.

. . .

Potato growers in coastal areas should try a trick used in Maine for decades. Dig a trench about six inches wide and six inches deep. Fill it with seaweed. Place chunks of seed potatoes at intervals of ten to twelve inches, then cover them with four to six inches of seaweed. At harvest time, pull back the seaweed and pick up the potatoes. There's none of that tiresome digging.

. . .

Save time when you **harvest asparagus.** Instead of cutting the spears from the bed, grab them firmly at the base and snap them near ground level. This causes less damage to the plant and assures that all you pick is tender enough to eat. You will avoid injury to emerging spears by not cutting below the ground, as was once recommended. (That practice is to the advantage of the commercial grower, as it improves the keeping qualities of asparagus, but we homegrowers rush it from garden to pot, anyway, right?) Harvest asparagus every day during the season. Once you let some stalks open into ferns, the harvest diminishes.

. . .

In warm regions, let three or four mother stalks of asparagus grow up from each plant after the harvest. Then sneak a second season by breaking off some of the new spears that emerge later on.

. . .

To **harvest rhubarb stalks,** hold near the bottom, twist and pull so that the stalk separates where it joins to the plant. Do not cut the stalks, or the juices will run from the cut, weakening the plant; and the remaining stalk will rot, inviting problems. "Red Valentine is better than the old green-stalked variety which turns gray when you cook it," suggests a rhubarb fan. To freeze, chop and put it in a bag — period. Rhubarb is a favorite among lazy gardeners — easy to grow, easy to harvest, pest free, and easy to freeze.

. . .

The **best keeper** among winter squashes is Butternut.

Triple-duty vegetables appeal to the lazy gardeners:

- Try Park's **Kuta squash.** Eat young like summer squash. Eat at midsize like eggplant. Eat at maturity like winter squash. It can be stored at this stage.
- Plant Burpee's Triple Treat **pumpkins,** good for jack-o-lanterns, pies, and high-protein snacks from the hull-less seeds. You can eat the seeds raw or roasted. To prepare, scoop them out, wash, and separate from fiber. Spread thinly on paper towels and dry for a few days in a warm, airy place. To roast, toss two cups of seeds with one and a half tablespoons of oil and a sprinkling of salt and place in a 250°F oven until golden brown. Watch carefully and shake the pan every now and then.

You get three huge zucchini and search for recipes to use them up. Two loaves of zucchini bread and one cake later, you still have two huge zucchini. Here's where five minutes in the garden daily can save you hours later. **Pick zucchini every day.** When it's only finger-length, even before the blossom falls off, it is a gourmet's delight. Eat raw with a dip or throw thin, raw slices into salads. Sauté tender young rounds in garlic and olive oil and sprinkle with parmesan cheese. Pickle whole or vertically sliced young zucchini, using a garlic-dill recipe.

• • •

If zucchini does get ahead of you, grate it finely (a food processor makes quick work of this), squeeze hard to eliminate as much liquid as possible, bag in one-cup portions, and freeze to use later in soups.

• • •

You're **growing cauliflower,** and you're too lazy to tie leaves over the forming head to keep it white? Partially break a few leaves and let them rest on the developing head, for easy blanching.

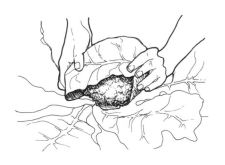

Break cauliflower leaves for easy blanching.

Young spinach — the younger the better — is delectable in salads or quickly stir-fried or steamed. Eat as much as you can when it's little.

• • •

When **harvesting cabbage,** cut the head instead of pulling the plant out of the ground. You may get another crop of smaller heads.

• • •

Cut six to eight inches of stem with the main head of **broccoli** to encourage production of lateral heads. Don't discard that stem when you cook the broccoli. Peel off the tough outer skin and, when steamed, it is just as tender as the florets. Always harvest broccoli when florets are in tight bud. Never let a yellow flower show its face.

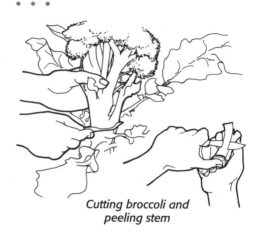

Cutting broccoli and peeling stem

• • •

Chinese cabbage likes cool weather. To get it to head in heat, loosely tie up all but the outer eight leaves. Do this about one month after seedlings are set out in the garden.

• • •

The **greens** of those beet seeds you broadcast in a wide row can be picked clean a section at a time. Pull, line up a handful, and snip off the roots with shears.

• • •

Too lazy to shell peas? Grow **edible-podded snap peas** instead, for plump peas (with pod) without the work of shelling. Pick, string, and steam or stir-fry briefly, until the pods turn bright green, and eat while still crunchy. Or blanch for one minute and freeze. Steam or sauté just enough to warm them up when you take them out of the freezer.

Too lazy to cook them? They're wonderful raw — just remove the strings. You can have your salad right out there at the vine, or wait until you cut them up and add to early lettuce. Eat them raw like carrots, serve with a dip, or take on picnics as finger food.

Too lazy to string them? Let the eaters do it, as they would shell cold, cooked shrimp.

THE RIGHT WAY TO STRING PEAS

If you **string edible-podded snap peas,** there's a right way and a wrong way, says Eleanor Kolkebeck. The right way can save many minutes. The wrong way produces broken strings, wasted time, and a frustrated harvester.

The right way: Start at the stem end. With a sharp paring knife, cut through the pod just below the cap toward the outside curve and pull off the string down to the tip. Next, cut through the tip and pull the string on the inside curve. It's important to do the outside part first, or the string won't come off in one piece.

Save time when you process snap beans. Cut off only the stem end. The tip tastes perfectly fine, so why bother to cut it off?

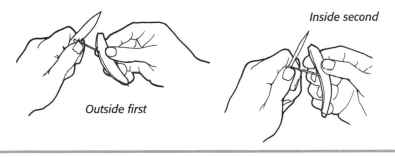

Inside second

Outside first

• • •

Never twist eggplants or peppers off the mother plant. Cut or snip off with knife or shears, and leave a short stem on each fruit.

• • •

Don't pull kohlrabi. To avoid disturbing remaining plants, just cut off below the "bulb" with a sharp knife.

• • •

If **Patty Pan squash** just don't seem to be worth the effort you're putting into growing them, perhaps you're harvesting them at the wrong time. Pick them when they're no more than three inches in diameter. That way they're delicious.

• • •

"There's nothing better than a sun-ripened tomato," exults a lazy gardener, "but nothing worse than reaching out to pick one and ending up with a handful of mush, because the mice or rabbits got there first." She picks just before the height of ripeness to **foil the varmints.**

Before a killing frost arrives, harvest all tomatoes except the tiny ones. Cut the fruits off the vine, leaving two inches of stem on each. The extra time it takes to do this will ensure better flavor after ripening. The tomatoes must be kept in a cool (45 to 50°F), dark — this is important — place. Wrap each one separately in newspaper. Check frequently, for a supply of tomatoes through Thanksgiving.

• • •

Your harvest of snap beans is prolific. You've already put enough in the freezer to last the winter. You've eaten all you can fresh. What to do with the rest? **Make dilly beans** for crunchy winter snacks. They're great Christmas gifts for your neighbors, and best of all, they're quick and easy.

Dilly Beans

4 lbs. green beans, whole (about 4 qts.)	$1/2$ tsp. (per pint jar) dill seed
$1/4$ tsp. (per pint jar) hot red pepper, crushed	1 clove garlic (per pint jar)
	5 sprigs fresh dill (per pint jar)
$1/2$ tsp. (per pint jar) whole mustard seeds	5 cups vinegar
	5 cups water
	$1/2$ cup salt

Wash beans thoroughly; drain and cut into lengths to fill pint jars. Pack beans into clean, hot jars; add pepper, mustard seed, dill seeds, garlic, and fresh dill. Combine vinegar, water, and salt; heat to boiling. Pour boiling liquid over beans, filling to $1/2$ inch of top of jar. Adjust lids. Process in boiling-water bath for five minutes. Remove jars, and if you are using jars with clamp tops, complete seals. Set jars upright, several inches apart, on a wire rack, to cool. Makes about 7 pints.

• • •

Lazy gardeners, here's an opportunity to sit in the shade and **watch thousands work** for you. Try beekeeping. Bees love to work, and you'll see a steady stream of the worker (fcmale) bees rushing in and out of the hive from dawn to dark, storing honey and pollinating blossoms in your garden and orchard. To get all this, plus 100 or so pounds of honey each year, you'll have to put in about six hours of work a year. Chances are you may spend more time than this with your bees as you get fascinated by the complex social structure that develops in the hive.

You think about edible flowers and you think, Ugh. But not if those flowers are **chives**. Tuck some in a flower bed, preferably the flower bed nearest the kitchen door, and enjoy the lovely lavender blossoms. Throw a few in your salad bowl for beauty and a mild oniony taste.

• • •

Be adventurous and let your **nasturtiums** do double-duty as pest-repellents and gay additions to the salad bowl. Leaves and flowers have a spicy, delicately pungent flavor similar to cress. At potluck suppers, I can always spot a salad brought by my neighbor, Catherine Osgood Foster, author and organic gardener. The artistically arranged garnish of red, orange, and yellow nasturtium blossoms is her trademark.

• • •

Don't grumble at the zucchini and squash; eat their blossoms before they have a chance to overburden you with produce. Cooks often use the male blossoms, which can be recognized by their long stems. Add to soup, sauté, dip in batter and deep-fry; or stuff with rice, meat, or cream cheese and bake.

• • •

Harness the sun's heat to help **ripen cantaloupes.** Place a flat stone under melons to absorb heat and help them ripen more evenly. No turning necessary.

• • •

For **earlier watermelons,** pinch out blossoms formed after the first two or three fruits are set, or prune the main vine to encourage side shoots, which set fruit earlier. Make sure the watermelon you worked so hard to grow is ripe before you harvest it:

- Thump it. It should sound hollow.
- Look at the rind. It should be yellow where it touches the ground.
- Inspect the tendrils at the joint just above the melon stem. They should be brown.

Ready to harvest? Cut (don't pull) it from the vine, with a short stem still attached to the melon.

Make cut flowers last longer by filling vases with **only 4 inches of water.** Oxygen is present in large quantities in the top 4-inches of water. Below that the water becomes depleted of oxygen and a smelly soup soon forms in the vase.

• • •

Take your **two-week vacation in August,** for best gardening results. By that time your vegetables will be large enough to compete with the weeds, and you won't return to a jungle of intruders hiding a few defeated vegetables. You will miss harvesting some of your vegetables at their prime, unless you time your planting schedule carefully.

• • •

Houseplants of vacationers will survive for a week or two if encased in plastic. If you plan to be away longer, try this:

- Soak houseplants well with fish emulsion.
- Sink into the ground in a shady place.
- Cover rims of pots with a little soil.
- Cut back some of the foliage on each houseplant.

Your plants may surprise you by thriving in your absence.

When to Prune

The basic pruning rule of thumb is to **give the plant three months of growing time between the time you cut it and when you expect it to bloom.** Months of dormancy do not count.

Try **pruning fruit trees in summer,** instead of in spring, when you are overloaded with planting. Remove all but one inch of new growth of non-fruiting wood. Leave a cluster of three to five leaves at the base. Do this when the base of the new shoot gets woody. This pruning dwarfs the tree, making for easier picking, encourages the development of fruit spurs for larger yields, and gets rid of most of the aphids on new growth.

SHRUBS TO BE PRUNED AFTER BLOOMING

The best time to prune these shrubs that bloom on year-old wood is just after the blossoms have faded. Then the shrub will grow new branches and form the buds that will bloom the following year.

Akebia

Amelanchier (shadblow)

Azalea

Benzoin (spice bush)

Berberis (barberry)

Buddleia alternifolia (butterfly bush)

Calycanthus floridus (sweet shrub, strawberry shrub)

Caragana (Siberian pea)

Celastrus (bittersweet)

Cercis (Judas tree, redbud)

Chaenomeles (flowering quince)

Chionanthus (white fringe)

Cornus (dogwood, without berries)

Cotinus coggyria (smoke tree)

Crataegus oxyacantha (English hawthorne)

Cydonia (Japanese quince)

Cytisus (broom)

Daphne (garland flower)

Deutzia

Exochorda (pearlbush)

Forsythia (goldenbell)

Hydrangea hortensia

Jasminum (jasmine)

Kalmia (laurel)

Kerria japonica (Japanese rose)

Kolwitzia amabilis (beautybush)

Lonicera fragrantissima (bush honeysuckle)

Magnolia

Philadelphus (mock-orange)

Physocarpus (ninebark)

Pieris (andromeda)

Potentilla (cinquefoil)

Prunus (flowering almond, cherry, plum)

Rhododendron

Ribes (flowering currant)

Rosa

Spirea (bridal wreath)

Spirea thunbergii

Spirea van Houtei

Syringa (lilac)

Tamarix (spring-flowering)

Viburnum carlesi, V. lantana (snowball)

Viburnum opulus (highbush cranberry)

Weigela

Shrubs that form flowers on wood grown the same season should be pruned when the plant is dormant.

Abelia x *grandiflora*

Abelia schumannii

Acanthopanax (five-leaved aralia)

Althea, shrubby (Rose of Sharon)

Amorpha (indigo bush)

Aralia elata (Japanese angelica)

Artemisia (sagebrush, southernwood, wormwood)

Baccharis (groundsel shrub)

Berberis (barberry)

Buddleia (butterfly bush, except for *B. alternifolia*)

Callicarpa (beautyberry)

Caryopteris (bluebeard)

Ceanothus

Cephalanthus (buttonbush)

Clethra (sweet pepper bush)

Cytisus nigricans (broom)

Dievilla sessilifolia (bush honeysuckle)

Euonymus kiautschovica (spreading euonymus)

Fatsia japonica (Japanese fatsia)

Franklinia alatamaha (Franklin tree)

Garrya (silk-tassel)

Hamamelis virginiana (witch hazel)

Hibiscus

Holodiscus discolor (ocean-spray)

Hydrangea arborescens 'Grandiflora'

Hydrangea paniculata 'Grandiflora'

Hypericum (St. Johnswort)

Indigofera (indigo)

Kerria

Lagerstroemia (crape myrtle)

Lespedeza (bush clover)

Ligustrum (privet)

Lilac japonica (tree lilac)

Lonicera (berried honeysuckle)

Lycium (matrimony vine)

Rhamnus frangula (alder, buckthorn)

Rhus (sumac, smoke tree)

Roses (garden bush varieties)

Rubus odoratus (flowering raspberry)

Salix (willow)

Salvia greggii (autumn sage)

Sambucus canadensis (American elder)

Sorbaria (false spirea)

Spiraea (all summer-blooming spirea)

Staphylea (bladdernut)

Stephanandra

Symphoricarpos (coralberry, snowberry)

Tamarix odessana (late-flowering tamarisk)

Viburnum (berry-bearing)

Vitex (chaste tree)

Berry-Picking Time

Leave two hands free for harvesting raspberries, blackberries, and highbush blueberries. Tie the gathering bucket around your waist. Pick more berries in less time.

• • •

Don't bother to wash raspberries. It makes them soggy and is a waste of time. Just eat.

• • •

Pick strawberries early in the day for best keeping. Sit down on the job instead of reaping an aching back. Rig up a seat that you can tie around your waist with a belt. Use an old stool and cut the legs down to three or four inches. Staple loops of webbing or rope to the seat to hold a belt. Or use a dairy farmer's "milking seat."

A strawberry-picking stool makes for a comfortable harvest.

• • •

If your idea of lazy gardening is to have **one major harvest** of the entire strawberry crop, order all plants of the same variety. "This year I bought sixty plants, half of one variety and half of another," says a gardener who strives for no wasted motion in his garden. "I wish I'd ordered just one kind. It seems as though I've been picking strawberries forever."

• • •

Do you have **everbearing raspberries?** Are you like the gardener who has had it with berry picking by the time he has finished harvesting one hundred and ten quarts of strawberries, and bing, suddenly the raspberries are ripe — red rubies that won't wait even a day beyond readiness to be picked? If you can't face picking under a merciless July sun, eliminate next year's summer bearing and have the luxury of picking bug-free berries in cool fall weather. Mow down to the ground *all* the canes in fall, even this year's new ones that would ordinarily produce your next July crop. Let the plants put all their strength into next summer's new canes, for a more vigorous, and probably earlier, fall crop at their tips. You also save the tedious work of cutting out only this summer's bearing canes, which die after harvest. It's much less time-consuming to mow down everything. Skeptical? Try it on half your bed.

• • •

For an **unusual treat,** plant golden raspberries and prune for a fall crop only. They'll bear from September first through October. A believer claims they're larger and meatier than reds, with a peachlike flavor.

Storage and Such

Freezing Tips

Freeze green beans whole to prevent sogginess. Blanch in boiling water for three minutes, cool in ice water, and blot dry before freezing.

• • •

Chop or slice onions and green pepper and **freeze raw.** Toss into cooked dishes straight from the freezer.

• • •

To **quick-freeze berries,** pour them, unwashed if possible, or well-drained, on a cookie sheet and pop into the freezer. When frozen, spoon into small plastic bags or containers and return to freezer.

Blueberries are almost as good as fresh ones when thawed. Raspberries and strawberries lose their texture. Use them in a jiffy lunch for the working man or woman. In the morning, throw one-half cup frozen raspberries or strawberries, one tablespoon honey, and one cup plain yogurt into a container. Stick it into the refrigerator at work. By lunch time, the berries will be thawed. Stir vigorously and enjoy the rich flavor of summer berries on a snowy day.

Cucumbers and zucchini don't freeze well. Take five minutes to pick them while they're young and little, slice thinly, and dry them for mid-winter snacks. It's especially easy if you live in a dry, sunny climate.

• • •

Freeze ripe tomatoes whole for use in cooking. Wash, dry, place in a plastic bag or container, and then freeze. When you need one, run cold water over it, and the skin will fall away. No need to struggle with immersion in boiling water and peeling before freezing.

• • •

Pick more vegetables than you'll eat for supper and freeze the extra each night. Avoids a marathon.

• • •

If you must **freeze spinach,** its bulk makes washing a messy chore. To keep from getting water and mud all over the kitchen, do the washing outdoors. Use a large washtub or a child's plastic swimming pool and the garden hose to make quick work of sand and soil imbedded in its crumply green leaves. Prop up on old screen on bricks, concrete blocks, or lumber, and let drippy spinach drain through it before heading back to the kitchen to blanch, cool, pack, and freeze.

The Many Uses of Herbs

Pick herbs before noon for the best taste. Use a food processor for effortless chopping of chives, parsley, basil, dill, chervil, fennel, marjoram, tarragon, and oregano. Freeze the excess in small amounts and pop frozen into cooked dishes for almost fresh flavor.

• • •

Throw some butter into your food processor with an herb to be chopped, for **quick herb butter.** Use on fish, meat, or breads.

• • •

To **dry herbs** you can:

- Spread them out loosely on screens or paper in a warm, dark attic.
- Hang in perforated paper bags.
- Dry in a 100°F oven, with the door left ajar. Spread out thinly.
- Hang in bunches in the refrigerator for a week to ten days. They will be nice and dry, flavorful, and still have excellent color.

• Use the microwave. Place a few herbs on a paper towel and microwave them for a minute or so.

When leaves are crisp, strip them off stems and put in closed containers. Small glass jars (baby-food size) are best. (Each time you open a jar, you lose aroma.) Store in a dry, cool, dark place.

* * *

Harvest basil before cool weather arrives. The flavor of its leaves is best before nighttime temperatures drop below 50°F.

* * *

Keep basil cut so it doesn't flower, but if you miss, use the blossoms for vinegar. In fact, **herb vinegars** are a convenient way to use herbs you're too lazy to dry or freeze, and they make wonderful gifts. Save interestingly shaped bottles from wine or other liquids. Use lots of herbs. Heat vinegar until hot but not boiling. Pour over herbs in a glass or ceramic container. Let sit for two to three weeks. Decant into bottles, filtering through Chemex paper. Use cider vinegar for all herbs except opal (red) basil and chive-blossom vinegar. Good herbs for vinegars are tarragon, dill, marjoram, sage, and thyme.

* * *

"I never have enough artemisia for wreaths, so this year I've planted it all around the inside of my garden fence. It keeps grass from getting into the garden and gives me a bountiful harvest," says Alice Moir, maker of herb wreaths. "**Never cut artemisia before September** first, or it turns an ugly gray. Cut later and it retains a silver look. After cutting, lay it carefully against the inside walls of bushel baskets to dry, and it will be molded into a rounded form for easier wreathmaking."

* * *

Grow lavender in a rocky, dry, sunny place (with plenty of lime) where other plants would gasp for water. Enjoy its blossoms all summer, then dry them for sachets. After you strip the stems, use the dry sticks in your fireplace or wood stove for a lovely fragrance.

* * *

Hate the smell of moth balls? Their fumes are not healthy for humans to inhale, anyway. Harvest and dry part of your herb garden to stuff into bags and hang in closets as a moth repellent. Combine santolina, tansy, and southernwood — much nicer than moth balls, and good for gifts, too. You can also add camphor, Roman wormwood, costmary, silver artemisia, mint, scented geraniums, lemon balm, lemon verbena, a bit of clove, and a bay leaf.

Long Life for Root Crops

If you have a **root cellar,** keep it cool in the fall when it's full of produce by opening ventilators on brisk nights and closing them on warm, sunny days. That's an easy way to keep the temperature and humidity at ideal levels.

• • •

Choose to grow thin-necked varieties of **onions** rather than thick-necked ones, and you'll have less incidence of-onion-neck rot in storage. Cure them in sun for a week or two after harvest, then lay screens in the rafters of your garage or attic and spread the onions one layer thick. Leave them there for a month or so. Make sure onion necks are thoroughly dry before clipping to an inch or two. Store in a cool, dry place with good ventilation.

• • •

Recall the lazy gardener's rule: Never do today what may never have to be done. You can dig your **carrots** in the fall, knock the dirt off them, cut the tops off, let them air for a day or two, bed them down with layers of peat moss, and then dig them out of the peat moss to eat them. Or you can fluff up a foot-deep layer of straw or hay over your wide row or raised bed of carrots, letting that layer reach out beyond the row by a foot.

When a hunger for carrots strikes you, lift up the hay and dig or pull out just the number you want. You'll find the carrots are crisp and even more flavorful than they were in the fall. But don't let them just sit there in the spring, or they will spoil.

One last thought: Mark the row with a couple of stakes. It's surprising how easy it is to lose a whole row of carrots if the snow gets to be a foot or two deep.

• • •

If you want those **carrots stored** in the house, place them in plastic bags with holes cut in them, and keep them in the refrigerator or some other cold — but not freezing — place.

Parsnips, too, can be left to winter over with a covering of hay. Make sure you dig them in spring before the tops begin to sprout. Their sweetness is intensified by cold storage in the ground.

• • •

Storing potatoes is hard work, but worth it. Cleaning out rotted potatoes is miserable work and ought to be avoided. The **secret to successful storage** is to keep the potatoes in a cool, well-ventilated area, and to keep the humidity as low as possible, and the potatoes dry.

Fighting Fall Frosts

Kale not only withstands frost, its **flavor is improved** with each chill. Twist off outer leaves as needed, before they become heavy and tough. Mulch with a foot of loose straw or hay if you're in a frigid winter climate and continue to harvest all winter.

• • •

If you were too lazy to get your plants covered before that **early fall frost,** don't write off your crops. Spray with a fine mist early in the morning, before sun hits the leaves, and you may earn a reprieve for your plants. Most damage after frost occurs when leaves warm up too fast in the sunshine. If you can thaw them with cool water first, they may survive.

Crisp Apples

If you pick or buy a lot of apples in the fall, you face a problem: how to **keep them fresh** for as many weeks as possible. Try getting them cold on a brisk fall night, then storing them in inexpensive styrofoam coolers. Apples tend to dry out when stored in a refrigerator; stored in these coolers, they retain that moisture, and their crisp freshness.

Get a Jump on Spring

A **late planting of lettuce** can be wintered over. Just cover with a foot or so of loose hay. Do the same with parsley for an early spring supply. It will have a stronger flavor then, but will keep you in fresh parsley until a new planting is ready.

• • •

In **northern climates,** where the ground stays frozen all winter, try a planting of peas in fall, after the ground has frozen. Get a big jump on the next growing season.

When autumn leaves fall, run the rotary mower over them before you rake, to reduce their volume and combat matting and blowing. Use them everywhere — rototill into the vegetable garden, apply lightly around evergreens and shrubs, dig into future tree holes, and add to the compost pile. You can probably even get bagged leaves from your unwise neighbors.

• • •

In the fall, take two hours of a Saturday afternoon as time to **get ready for spring.** If you have a tiller, drain the gasoline from it, drop a few drops of oil into the cylinder, and even change the oil, so come warm weather, when things are rushing, you'll be ready to till.

• • •

If you won't have to bother with spring tilling because you mulch year-round, use that same Saturday afternoon to plan and **mark the rows** for next year's garden, and you'll be all ready for spring planting the minute the soil is.

• • •

Clean, repair, and **sharpen your tools** before hanging them up for the last time. Take inventory and jot down Christmas present requests to fill your needs.

Winter Protection

Have you shrubs or perennials that are borderline hardy? A New Hampshire gardener placed large rocks to the northwest of his tender heathers on a south-facing bank. In summer, the rocks add a pleasing design element to the garden. In winter, they absorb the sun's heat in the day and retain some of that heat at night. They also protect the plants from chill northwest winds.

• • •

Put bales of hay around **tender plants** to protect them in winter.

• • •

Strawberry plants need **winter protection.** Save weeding headaches next season by using a weed-free winter mulch, such as pine needles. You can give the plants a dusting of mulch after the first few light frosts, but wait until the temperature drops to 20°F before applying it to a depth of three or four inches. By this time, plants will have hardened off. Remove mulch in the spring, but keep it in the alleys between the plants to do double duty as weed-smotherer and as a handy covering for blossoms when a late frost threatens.

Fresh Sprouts: The Perfect Winter Crop

Lazy gardeners, here's a crop that has no weeds or insect pests, needs no soil, grows in any kind of weather, and is ready for harvest in two to five days. Grow your own sprouts in winter, for a continuing supply of high-vitamin greens. All you need to invest is a minute or two a day for rinsing.

Use seeds that have not been chemically treated. Try a variety: mung beans, alfalfa, parsley, watercress, mustard, soybeans, lentils, peas, flax, and cereal grains such as wheat, oats, barley, or rye. (Never eat potato and tomato sprouts. Members of the nightshade family, they are poisonous.) As they sprout, seeds soar in nutritional value. One-half cup of sprouted soybeans contains vitamin C equal to six glasses of orange juice. Oat sprouts are high in vitamin E. As sprouts grow, vitamin B-complex soars.

To sprout seeds, you need a wide-mouthed jar. Cover it with cheesecloth and a rubber band, or buy plastic-screened sprouting covers that screw on wide-mouthed canning jars. You need two table-spoons of seeds to a quart jar.

1. Wash seeds in water.
2. Soak overnight in a warm, dark place — one part seeds to three parts warm water.
3. In the morning, remove floating seeds. They're sterile. Pour off liquid and save it for soup.
4. Rinse seeds in warm water and drain.
5. Lay jar on its side in a warm closet. (You may want to put a towel or a pan under it to catch any drips.)
6. Rinse three times a day until ready for eating. Keep in the refrigerator after that.

Alfalfa seeds take four to five days to maturity. Leave in indirect sunlight the last day to green up. Mung beans take five days.

Wheatberries and lentils are best after three days, and hulled sunflower seeds are ready when barely sprouted, just one day old.

Be sure to wash jars and screens thoroughly between batches with hot, soapy water, to prevent bacterial contamination.

How do you eat sprouts? Munch on raw sprouts at snack time, toss them in salads, mix with cottage cheese, add to sandwiches instead of lettuce, or sprinkle on soup. Stir-fry or steam them as a cooked vegetable, mix with rice, or add to scrambled eggs and omelets.

Keep winter doldrums at bay with this easiest of crops, and dream of spring, when seeds in dark earth will again sprout in your garden.

Index

Page references in *italics* indicate illustrations; **bold** indicates charts.

Cucumbers
  and beetles, 104
  and compost, 20–21, 71
  and corn, 70
  drying, 127
  planting, 39, 58
  staking, 54–55
Cucurbits, 6, 31

D

Dickey, Closey, 46, 78, 92
Dilly Beans (recipe), 120
Disease tips
  black spot, 106
  blossom end-rot, 103
  damping-off organisms, 44
  early blight, 106
  fire blight, 106
  mildew, 47, 106
  milky spore, 105
  rotting, 106
  scab, 31
  sunscald, 47, 103

E

Eggplants, 6, 20, 57–58, 71, 119

F

Fences, use of, 49, 53, 95–98
Fertilizers, 25, 34. *See also*
  Composting tips
Flowers
  cut, 122
  gardens, easy, 14
  harvesting, 113–14, 121–22
  perennials, 14, 81, 92, 113–14
  planting, 14, 81, 92
  staking, 55
Foster, Catherine Osgood, 121
Foster, Kit, 83
Foster, Tom, 47

Freezing tips, 126–27
Frost date averages, *37, 58*
Fruits
  blueberries, 31, 78, 90, 126
  harvesting, 115–16, 121, 125–26
  planting, 76–79
  pruning trees, 122
  raspberries, 76–77, 125–26
  strawberries, 31, 44, 77–78, 90,
    98–99, 125–26, 131–32
  trees and pests, 107–8

G

Gardening tips. *See also* Composting
    tips; Disease tips; Harvesting tips;
    Mulch tips; Pest tips; Planting tips;
    Soil tips; Tool tips; Watering tips;
    Weeding tips
  landscaping, easy, 11–13
  lawn basics, 11–13
  organization, 1–3, 35–36
  plot, perfect, 2
  pruning, 16, 122–24
  routines, time-saving, 3–4
  site, ideal, 4–6
  walkways, 7, 8, 11
  Gardening Without Work, 21
Garlic, 6, 58, 92

H

Harvesting tips
  berries, 125–26
  crop placement, 5
  flowers, 113–14, 121–22
  fruits, 115–16, 121, 125–26
  herbs, 127–28
  vegetables, 115–21
  yields, higher, 7, 10, 18, 47
Hay
  and composting, 26
  as mulch, 85, 88, 92

Plant stand (directions), 41–42
Plastic
  black, 62, 91, 100
  use of, 46, 58, 122
Potatoes, 31, 68, 116, 130
Potting mix (directions), 43
Pruning, 16, 122–24

R

Raised bed planting, 7–9, 15, 60–62,
  65, 96
Raspberries, 76–77, 125–26
Raymond, Dick, 60

S

Salad gardens, 5, 65–66
Seed tips
  broadcast, 7, 59, 62, 64–65
  damping-off organisms, 44
  germination, 42–43, 66
  hard-coated, 46
  overview, 38–39
  pelleted, 57, 65
  plant stand (directions), 41–42
  potting mix (directions), 43
  size of, 38
  soaking of, 66
  spacing, 44
  starting indoors, 41–46
  storage, 38
  tapes, 65
  thinning seedlings, 44
  tiny, planting of, 64–65
Shrubs, 28, **123–24**
Smith, Gerald, 27
Soil Conservation Service, 3
Soil tips. *See also* Composting tips
  clay soils, lightening, 30–31
  contaminated, 94
  cover crops, 18–20, 94
  and diseases, 95, 104

drainage, 4, 8, 26
humic acid, 18
hydrangea color, 33
pH, 25, 31–33, 95, 104
reasons for building, 17–18
tips, 33–34
Spinach, 58, 64, 66–67, 118, 127
Sprouts, 132–33
Square bed planting, 9–10, 62, 92
Squash, 20, 39, 58, 70–71, 121
Staking tips
  beans, 53–54
  cucumbers, 54–55
  flowers, 55
  overview, 36, 47–48, 56
  peas, 51–53
  tomatoes, 48–51
Stevenson, Nora, 84
Stout, Ruth, 21, 51, 66, 85, 92
Strawberries
  Alpine, 44
  and birds, 98–99
  harvesting, 125–26
  mulch, 90
  planting, 77–78
  winter protection, 131–32
Succession planting, 6

T

Tomatoes
  companion planting, 70
  and compost, 20, 71
  determinate, 48, 74
  diseases, 103
  freezing, 127
  harvesting, 119–20
  indeterminate, 48, 50
  planting, 58, 73–75
  self-fertilizing, 74
  staking, 48–51, 74
  transplanting, 46, 71

Other Storey Titles You Will Enjoy

The Big Book of Gardening Secrets, by Charles W.G. Smith. Provides scores of professional secrets for growing better vegetables, herbs, fruits, and flowers. 352 pages. Paperback. ISBN 1-58017-000-5.

Bugs, Slugs, & Other Thugs, by Rhonda Massingham Hart. Suggests hundreds of ways to stop pests without risk to the user or the environment. 240 pages. Paperback. ISBN 0-88266-664-9.

Carrots Love Tomatoes: Secrets of Companion Planting for Successful Gardening, by Louise Riotte. Explains how to put vegetable relationships to work for you in your garden to produce a bountiful crop. 224 pages. Paperback. ISBN 1-58017-027-7.

The Gardener's Weed Book, by Barbara Pleasant. Explains how to understand, identify, and control weeds using earth-safe methods. 144 pages. Paperback. ISBN 0-88266-921-4.

Let It Rot!, by Stu Campbell. Provides information on selecting and combining compost materials and simplifies the technical terminology to make composting easy. 160 pages. Paperback. ISBN 1-58017-023-4.

The Mulch Book, by Stu Campbell. Details how to make and use bark, stones, hay, compost, plastic sheeting, and other materials as a barrier for keeping weeds out and beneficial elements in. 160 pages. Paperback. ISBN 0-88266-659-2.

Roses Love Garlic: Companion Planting and Other Secrets of Flowers, by Louise Riotte. Provides secrets to successful "companion planting" and offers lore and growing advice for hundred of flowers. 256 pages. Paperback. ISBN 1-58017-028-5.

Secrets to Great Soil, by Elizabeth P. Stell. Shows how soil fertility affects gardens and how to evaluate your soil's texture, structure, pH, and general fertility. 224 pages. Hardcover. ISBN # 1-58017-009-9. Paperback. ISBN 1-58017-008-0.

These books and other Storey books are available at your bookstore, farm store, garden center, or directly from Storey Publishing, Schoolhouse Road, Pownal, Vermont 05261, or by calling 1-800-441-5700. www.storey.com.